HOLT

Elements of

Language

FIRST COURSE

Think as a Writer: Interactive Grammar WorkText

Grammar Practice for Chapters 1–19

- Choices Activities
- Literary Models
- Writing Applications
- Grammar Worksheets and Lessons

HOLT, RINEHART AND WINSTON

A Harcourt Education Company

Orlando • Austin • New York • San Diego • London

Printed in the United States of America

ISBN 978-0-03-099560-6
ISBN 0-03-099560-4

8 9 1409 14 13 12
4500382691

Table of Contents

Table of Contents *(continued)*

Table of Contents *(continued)*

Table of Contents *(continued)*

Table of Contents *(continued)*

Section 3: More Practice with Combining Sentences

About This Book

At the beginning of this workbook you will find reference sheets designed to help improve your writing by offering tips for correctly constructing sentences and paragraphs. Keep copies of these pages in your subject notebook and refer to them whenever you read or begin a writing assignment.

This workbook gives you practice in grammar to help you improve your writing skills. **Section 1: Applying Grammar, Usage, and Mechanics** gives you activities and writing applications to help you improve your grammar in your writing. The practice worksheets in **Section 2: Practice with Sentences and Paragraphs** and **Section 3: More Practice with Combining Sentences** will help you write correct sentences and give you help in combining sentences to make your writing more interesting.

Section 1: Applying Grammar, Usage, and Mechanics has the following features:

- **Choices Activities** These activities give you an opportunity to explore a topic in grammar in a way that interests you most. Art, math, creative writing, and more are used to help you learn grammar.
- **Literary Models** You will use a story to see why authors use the techniques they do, and you will write your own examples of authors' styles. These worksheets show the difference between creative writing and formal writing.
- **Writing and Proofreading Applications** These worksheets give you a writing activity and tips on how to complete the activity using the steps in the writing process, from prewriting to proofreading. The section also gives you ways to do more with your writing assignment. The proofreading applications give guidelines and practice to help you improve your writing.

Section 2: Practice with Sentences and Paragraphs and **Section 3: More Practice with Combining Sentences** contain worksheets to help you practice writing good sentences. Practice worksheets help you improve your writing by providing you with practice in the following:

- revising and proofreading
- combining sentences
- identifying fragments and run-ons
- identifying stringy and wordy sentences.

Writing different types of sentences and correcting bad sentences will make your writing more interesting.

Details and Supporting Sentences

KINDS OF DETAILS	SUPPORTING SENTENCES
Sensory Details	
Sight	The bright sun glared off the front windshield of the car.
Hearing	Thunder boomed down the canyon, echoing off the walls.
Touch	My hands felt frozen to the cold, steel handlebars.
Taste	Thirstily, she gulped down the sweet orange juice.
Smell	The sharp, unpleasant odor of asphalt met his nose.
Facts	In 2004 an earthquake caused at sunami that reached up to 80 feet high.
Examples	Fierce windstorms occur worldwide. For example, tornadoes have wind speeds over 200 miles per hour.

Transitional Words and Phrases

TRANSITIONAL WORDS AND PHRASES			
Comparing and Contrasting Ideas	also although and another	but however in the same way like	likewise similarly too yet
Showing Cause and Effect	as a result because	since	therefore
Showing Time	about after at before during finally	first, second, and so on immediately later meanwhile next often	soon then until when
Showing Place	above across among around before behind below	beneath beside between by down here in	into near next over there under
Showing Support	for example for instance	for this reason	in fact

Types of Paragraphs

Narrative used to tell a story or recount an event	Erik peered beneath the rock and saw a small stone. The stone had a metal ring attached to its center. Erik tugged at the ring and felt the stone move. He pulled harder. Suddenly, the rock lifted. Below it was a dark hole. Erik dropped a pebble down the hole and listened. He heard nothing.
Descriptive used to describe a scene or an object	The narrow front door opens right into the living room. At first the room seems gloomy. As your eyes adjust, you can pick out the many bright spots. The hooked rug in front of the door has reds and yellows in it. On the left wall is a small, blackened fireplace with a cheerful fire burning. Beyond that, two windows face the door. Their heavy curtains let in narrow columns of daylight. On the far side of the room, a tiny fern grows in the sun that streams through the third window.
Expository used to provide information, including facts, instructions, and definitions	Lay the square egg-roll skin on a table with one corner pointing toward you. Put a few spoonsful of filling in the center. Then, take the corner of the skin that is closest to you and fold it over the filling. Next, fold the two side corners inward, using both hands. Then, brush a little beaten egg onto the unfolded corner. Finally, roll the filled part up and over the last corner.
Persuasive used to share opinions and convince others to agree or take action	There are several good reasons for building a new light rail in our city. First, such a railway would reduce the air pollution and noise pollution, which have reached alarming levels. Second, the railway would decrease our parking problems and the traffic jams. Third, building and staffing the railway would create new jobs for the city's workers.

Symbols for Revising and Proofreading

Symbol	Example	Meaning of Symbol
≡	Tucker's homestyle Restaurant.	Capitalize a lowercase letter.
/	the City of Raleigh	Lowercase a capital letter.
^	a cup of milk	Insert a missing word, letter, or punctuation mark.
ℓ	How's the that apple?	Leave out a word, letter, or punctuation mark.
∽	frist	Change the order of letters or words.
¶	¶"Go ahead," he said.	Begin a new paragraph.
⊙	She wept⊙	Add a period.
^	I still apologized, however.	Add a comma.

Section 1: Applying Grammar, Usage, and Mechanics

NAME CLASS DATE

Choices: Exploring Sentences

Here's your chance to step out of the grammar book and into the real world. You may not notice them, but you and the people around you use parts of sentences every day. The following activities challenge you to find a connection between parts of sentences and the world around you. Do the activity below that suits your personality best, and then share your discoveries with your class. Have fun!

CRITICAL ANALYSIS

Everyone's a Critic

Writers love sentence fragments. Find five examples of published sentence fragments, and present them to the class. In each case, lead the class in evaluating whether the fragment or a complete sentence should have been used. Have a debate. You argue for the fragment while a friend argues for a sentence. Let the class be the judge.

DRAMA

Typical Types

Some people speak in sentence fragments quite often. However, some people are more comfortable using complete sentences. How would you describe these two types of people? How would a conversation between them sound? Write a dialogue between two such people. With a friend, tape your dialogue and play it for the class.

CREATIVE WRITING

Four by Four

Write four poems of four sentences each. In each poem, use the different types of sentences (declarative, imperative, interrogative, and exclamatory) once apiece.

DISCUSSION

On Location

While watching the news, have you ever noticed that no matter where a reporter goes in the world, he or she can find at least one person who speaks English? The reporter may even be in some tiny village in Somewhere, Planet Earth, speaking to a person who speaks English just about as well as anyone in Anywhere, U.S.A. What does this observation tell you about the value of English? Where can a knowledge of English take you? Do some research, and report your findings and observations to the class.

MATHEMATICS

X and Y equals Z

Start with ten mathematical equations. Then, translate these equations into sentences and label each subject and predicate. Include some examples showing compound subjects and compound verbs.

ART

Mr. or Ms. D. Clarative

Draw four or five characters. Each character should personify one kind of sentence. In other words, you'll draw one character each for declarative, interrogative, and exclamatory sentences, and one or two for imperative sentences. Name each character. (Yes, a label such as Mr. or Ms. D. Clarative would be acceptable.) Post your drawings in the classroom, and take a bow!

ORIGINAL PROJECTS

Take Charge

Be the one in charge! Create your own project. Begin by asking yourself what puzzles you about sentences. What would your classmates find interesting about sentences? If you're good at something or have a hobby, work it into your project. For instance, if you like dinosaurs, write a dialogue between dinosaurs and use every kind of sentence. How about a dialogue between two people in which one gives the subject and the other gives the predicate? You could make a multimedia presentation. Draw a chart. Discuss your plans with your teacher, sharpen your pencil, and charge ahead!

NAME ______________________ CLASS ______________ DATE ______________

Literary Model: Dialogue

When Cloyd was little, he used to talk to his sister about how badly he wanted to find his father, but she didn't seem to need to know him at all, so he had kept his dream inside. . . . Now here he was with his heart pounding, following the nurse down the long hallway to his father's room. . . .

"How did this happen?"

"Car accident," she said. "I don't know any details."

"How long has he been like this?"

"Four years."

"Are you sure he's Leeno Atcitty?"

"Yes, of course."

"Where's he from?"

"I think I heard that once . . . Utah, I think. Monument Valley. I wonder if this could be the man you were looking for."

—from *Bearstone* by Will Hobbs

EXERCISE A Underline each sentence fragment that appears in the above passage.

EXERCISE B

1. Rewrite the dialogue to eliminate all sentence fragments. That is, whenever you come to a sentence fragment, supply words that make it a complete sentence.

____

____

____

____

____

____

____

____

____

____

Literary Model (continued)

2. Read the original passage and your revision. Why do you think the author chose to write the dialogue as a mix of sentences and sentence fragments rather than using only complete sentences?

EXERCISE C Write a dialogue in which one person asks questions to try to help a friend who is upset. Have the upset friend speak mostly in sentence fragments to convey his or her feelings or emotions.

EXERCISE D

1. How does the character who uses sentence fragments sound different from the other character in your dialogue?

2. How would your dialogue sound different if both characters used only complete sentences?

NAME ______ CLASS ______ DATE ______

Writing Application: Letter

Writers use different types of sentences to convey different types of messages. When writers make statements, they use declarative sentences. When they ask questions, they use interrogative sentences.

DECLARATIVE Andrea is playing in the tennis tournament today.

INTERROGATIVE Where is the tournament being played?

Writing Activity

Your teacher has arranged for your class to write to students learning English in Denmark. Each student in your class has been assigned a Danish pen pal. Your assignment is to write a letter to your new pen pal. Using at least five declarative sentences, introduce yourself and tell your pen pal about life in the United States. Using at least five interrogative sentences, ask your pen pal questions about himself or herself and life in Denmark.

PREWRITING Think about what you would like to know about your pen pal, and make a list of your questions. Try to avoid asking only yes-or-no questions. Open-ended questions will give you more information. Your pen pal may have similar questions for you, so you can use your list to help you decide what to write about yourself. Think about what you would like to know about Denmark. What do you think your pen pal would want to know about the United States?

WRITING Decide how to organize your letter. You might tell about yourself in the first half of the letter and ask questions in the second half of the letter. Another way to write your letter is to alternate between telling about yourself and asking related questions about your pen pal. Since your pen pal is still learning English, he or she may not understand slang terms, so be careful with word choice.

REVISING Have a friend read your letter; then, discuss it. Is it interesting? Have you left out any important information about yourself? Can your friend think of any other questions that you should ask your pen pal?

PUBLISHING Check your paragraph for errors in spelling and punctuation. Does each declarative sentence end with a period? Does each interrogative sentence end with a question mark? With your teacher's permission, post your letter with your classmates' letters on the bulletin board. Find or create pictures that illustrate the area where your pen pal lives.

Extending Your Writing

You may wish to extend this activity by finding a real pen pal for yourself or your whole class. Your teacher may be able to help you find Internet sites that help classes from around the United States or around the world set up letter exchange programs. Not only would you get to practice your writing skills, but you would make new friends as well.

NAME CLASS DATE

Choices: Exploring Parts of Speech

Here's your chance to step out of the grammar book and into the real world. You may not notice them, but you and the people around you use the parts of speech every day. The following activities challenge you to find a connection between the parts of speech and the world around you. Do the activity below that suits your personality best, and then share your discoveries with your class. Have fun!

BUILDING BACKGROUND KNOWLEDGE

Every Letter Counts

Have a contest to determine who can find the longest proper compound noun. Entries must be verified in a reliable source such as a dictionary, an atlas, or an encyclopedia.

TIME LINE

First and Last

If you've got a first name and a last name, your name is a compound noun. Not everybody has a compound noun for a name, you know. Plato didn't, Aristotle didn't, and lots of other people don't. However, most people do. Make a time line that your class can use throughout the year. Leave room for additions. Then, pick out some of your favorite historical figures and write their names on the appropriate part of the time line. In small letters under each two-word name, write *compound noun*.

AUDITORY

Begin at the End

Have you noticed that nouns often have certain suffixes, such as *–tion*, *–ology*, and *–er*? Identify as many of these suffixes as you can. Then, get together with some friends and use your list of suffixes to make up ten new nouns! Here's a question to get you started: What's a good name for those colorful little erasers shaped like dinosaurs, hearts, and other things?

CHARACTERIZATION

Way Back When

Pick three historical periods (such as the Victorian era, medieval times, Ice Age, or Jazz Age). Choose at least ten adjectives that describe each of those time periods. Post your adjectives in the appropriate places on a time line.

COLLABORATIVE LEARNING

Betty the Boa Constrictor

There's a big difference between saying, "I took an animal with me," and "I took my pet boa constrictor Betty with me." *Animal* is a general noun that could refer to anything from an elephant to a tarantula. Choose a partner. Then, in a page or less, write a description of a day on safari, and use only general nouns. Then, trade papers with your partner, and revise the description so that every noun is a specific noun. Trade again, and compare results.

FOREIGN LANGUAGES

Las, Les, Der, and The

Why do we need articles, anyway? Do other languages use articles? How does Spanish use articles? German? Japanese? Find out about at least one other language. Interview someone who speaks another language, or conduct a library search. Then, write a one-page essay explaining how another language uses articles and comparing it with English. Read your essay to the class.

VISUAL PRESENTATION

Documentation

Get together with a group of friends or lead the class in a brainstorming session. Your goal is to make a poster listing nouns that name every kind of document that exists. Concentrate especially on documents that you and your friends are most likely to create in the future. Your list should include job application forms, personal letters, business cards, reports, recipes, and directions. Don't limit yourself to print media; try to include documents that can be produced in other media like DVDs, CDs, and electronic media. When you've finished your list, organize it into categories and create a poster to display in class.

Literary Model: Poem

Mama Is a Sunrise

When she comes slip-footing through the door,
she kindles us
like lump coal lighted,
and we wake up glowing.
She puts a spark even in Papa's eyes
and turns out all our darkness.

When she comes sweet-talking in the room,
she warms us
like grits and gravy,
and we rise up shining.
Even at nighttime Mama is a sunrise
that promises tomorrow and tomorrow.

—by *Evelyn Tooley Hunt*

EXERCISE A Underline the nouns in the above poem. Then, fill in the blanks below so that each noun is listed in its appropriate category. Note: Do not write the same noun twice in one category.

Common Nouns

____________ ____________ ____________ ____________

____________ ____________ ____________ ____________

____________ ____________

Proper Nouns

____________ ____________ ____________ ____________

EXERCISE B

1. A *metaphor* is a comparison between two unlike things in which one thing is said to be another thing. In the poem above, to what does the poet compare the character Mama? (Hint: Your response to Exercise A should contain the answer.)

____

____

2. What do you think the poet is trying to communicate about Mama and the impression that she has on her family? How do words such as "lump coal" and "grits and gravy" support the poet's characterization of Mama?

____

____

Literary Model (continued)

EXERCISE C

1. Choose a family member to be the subject of a poem. At the top of the following space, write the name of the family member. Reflect on him or her for a few minutes. Then, thinking in terms of one or more metaphors, brainstorm a list of nouns that relate to this person and write them under the name. You will use some or all of these nouns in the poem. As Evelyn Tooley Hunt did, try to include nouns that have an unusual connection to a human being.

2. Write the poem on the lines below.

EXERCISE D How did you use nouns to describe the family member? Why did you use these particular nouns and not any others?

Writing Application: Journal Entry

When writers use common nouns, they could be referring to any member of a general group. Sometimes, though, writers want to name a specific person, place, thing, or idea. To do this, writers use proper nouns. Substituting proper nouns for common nouns can make nearly any piece of writing more memorable.

GENERAL The girl lives in the city.

SPECIFIC Judy Martin lives in San Francisco.

In the first sentence, the common noun *girl* does not name a young female in particular. It could refer to any girl, just as the common noun *city* could refer to any city. In the second sentence, the proper noun *Judy Martin* tells exactly whom the author means, and the proper noun *San Francisco* tells exactly where she lives. Notice that proper nouns are capitalized.

WRITING ACTIVITY

Your class is gathering material for a time capsule to be opened in a hundred years. Your teacher has asked you and your classmates each to write a journal entry describing the everyday life of a student. Your journal entry will be a historical document when it is unearthed in a hundred years. Historians look for the specific names of people, places, things, and ideas when studying the past. To give the historians a clear picture of your life, include at least ten proper nouns in your journal entry. For example, provide interesting details about your friends, your school, your neighborhood, or your favorite books and music.

PREWRITING You cannot include every moment of the day in your journal entry, so make a list of the highlights of your day. Think of details that you can add to flesh out events and personalize your description.

WRITING Decide how to organize your journal entry. For example, you could write about events in chronological order. Another option is to arrange topics by subject. However you decided to organize your entry, do not just list events, but create a narrative with smooth transitions between topics.

REVISING Read through your journal entry, pretending that it was written by a stranger. Do you gain a sense of what a day in this "other person's" life was like? If not, what is missing?

PUBLISHING Check your journal entry for errors in spelling and punctuation. Remember to capitalize all proper nouns. Compare your journal entry with those of your classmates. Are your experiences similar? What specific things do you have in common? What specific things are different? After you and your classmates have compared journal entries, consider including your journal entries in a real time capsule.

EXTENDING YOUR WRITING

You may wish to develop this writing exercise further. You might write about your personal opinions or reactions to current events, making sure to choose events that you think people might be interested in a hundred years from now. Or you might write down your guesses as to what everyday life will be like a hundred years from now.

NAME CLASS DATE

Choices: Investigating Parts of Speech

Here's your chance to step out of the grammar book and into the real world. You may not realize it, but people around you use parts of speech every day. The following activities challenge you to find a connection between parts of speech and the world around you. Do the activity below that suits your personality best, and then share your discoveries with your class. Have fun!

RESEARCH/ETYMOLOGY

Deep Roots

Look up the etymologies of the words that name these parts of speech—*verb, adverb, preposition, conjunction*, and *interjection*. Where and when did these words originate? What are their roots? If it is available in your school library, check the *Oxford English Dictionary*. Present your research to your classmates, and pass out copies of your findings. Post appropriate notes on a time line.

LINGUISTICS

Staples, Hinges, and Glue

Conjunction is a pretty cool word, but maybe you can think of a better one. With a friend, brainstorm some new names for the coordinating conjunctions. First, think about what conjunctions do. Then, ask yourself what other things join things together. Are these joints permanent or temporary? How strong are they? Then, tell your classmates about your new terminology.

CREATIVE WRITING

Who Am I?

If you could bring the parts of speech to life, how would you make them act? If you were an interjection, what would you be like? Would you prefer philosophy or sports? Would you be organized and calm or impulsive and emotional? Write a personality profile for three parts of speech. Then, share (or perform) your profiles.

VISUAL LEARNING

Apples to Oranges

Who says you can't compare apples to oranges? Use colors to code the parts of speech in a paragraph. Then, choose a famous poem and color-code it. When you show your code to the class, also tell them which task (color-coding the paragraph or color-coding the poem) was harder.

PERFORMANCE

Walk On

Have you ever heard the words *traipse* and *sashay*? They are both synonyms for *walk*. Use a thesaurus to look up the word *walk*. Make a list of all the synonyms. Then, show your classmates that adverbs aren't the only words that show *how*. The right verb can do the job, too. Demonstrate how to walk in at least five different ways.

MATHEMATICS

The X Factor

Consider the following questions as you write a one-page essay that compares math to grammar: In mathematics, what elements of equations or formulas could function as parts of speech? For instance, what part of speech would a number be? How about a plus sign? Choose several math symbols, and tell whether each of your choices acts like a certain part of speech. Explain your comparisons to the class.

SPORTS REPORTING

It's *How* That Counts

What would sports reporting be without adverbs? Write a newspaper account of a sporting event at your school. First, write the account without using any adverbs. Then, revise the account to include as many adverbs as you can without sounding silly. Which version is easier to write? Don't forget the headline (and the byline)!

ORIGINAL PROJECT

Mix and Match

Make up your own project. Illustrate transitive verbs, draw a cartoon of a preposition and a verb having a conversation, develop an electronic slide show, use a Venn diagram to compare transitive and intransitive verbs, or invent some other project. Be sure to get your teacher's permission.

NAME CLASS DATE

for **CHAPTER 3: PARTS OF SPEECH OVERVIEW** *pages 100–103*

Literary Model: Using Adverbs in a Description

The opinions of this club were completely controlled by Nicholas Vedder, a patriarch of the village, and landlord of the inn, at the door of which he took his seat from morning till night, just moving sufficiently to avoid the sun and keep in the shade of a large tree; so that the neighbors could tell the hour by his movements as accurately as by a sundial. It is true he was rarely heard to speak, but smoked his pipe incessantly. His adherents, however, perfectly understood him, and knew how to gather his opinions. When anything that was read or related displeased him, he was observed to smoke his pipe vehemently, and to send forth short, frequent, and angry puffs; but when pleased, he would inhale the smoke slowly and tranquilly, and emit it in light and placid clouds; and sometimes, taking the pipe from his mouth, and letting the fragrant vapor curl about his nose, would gravely nod his head in token of perfect approbation.

—from "Rip Van Winkle" by Washington Irving

EXERCISE A List ten adverbs that appear in this passage.

EXERCISE B

1. Underline the adverbs in the passage. Then, read the passage aloud, leaving the adverbs out.
2. Explain how leaving adverbs out changes the description. Is it better with the adverbs or without them?

Literary Model (continued)

EXERCISE C Imagine that you are at a park with a younger sibling, cousin, or other relative. Write a paragraph in which you describe his or her actions. Use several adverbs in your description.

EXERCISE D

1. Rewrite your paragraph, leaving out the adverbs.

2. How is your paragraph affected by deleting the adverbs?

Writing Application: Personal Description

Adverbs come quickly to the writer's aid when verbs, adjectives, and even other adverbs need further clarification. In fact, speakers often use them without even thinking about it. In writing, however, replace overused adverbs like *really, very,* and so when you can.

OVERUSED ADVERB The athletes performed really well.

FRESHER ADVERB The athletes performed brilliantly.

Writing Activity

This year, the school's yearbook staff has come up with a fun idea. During English class, each student will write a paragraph for a "Where Are They Now?" chapter in the yearbook. Imagine yourself ten years in the future. Where will you be? What will you have accomplished? Imagine yourself ten years from now, and write an optimistic paragraph for your peers to read. Describe your future self with at least five carefully chosen adverbs.

PREWRITING Find some quiet, uninterrupted time to imagine yourself ten years from now. High school will be behind you—what were you known for during those years? After high school, will you go to college, start a career, begin a family? Since you're imagining, imagine the best life you can. Jot down the possible futures as you allow yourself to think ahead.

WRITING You only have one paragraph in which to share your dreams with your friends, so choose your favorite future from your prewriting. Describe the future in third person, writing about yourself as someone else might. Although you are writing only one paragraph, organize it well, as if it were an essay in miniature. Decide on the best order for the facts about yourself.

REVISING Now that you have the basic paragraph structure, add clarifying detail to your description. Use at least five strong, specific adverbs—no weak *really, very,* or *so* for this stellar report on your life!

PUBLISHING Check your paragraph for errors in punctuation and spelling. But why wait until the yearbook comes out to share your paragraph and read others' dreams? With your teacher's permission, make a bulletin board display with paragraphs and pictures.

Extending Your Writing

This exercise could lead to a more developed writing project. In two or three years, you will leave your current school and head to high school. Write a personal essay in which you outline the goals you would like to accomplish by that time. In your concluding paragraph, set a few distant goals for your high school years, too.

NAME ________________ CLASS ________ DATE ________

Choices: Exploring Complements

Here's your chance to step out of the grammar book and into the real world. You may not notice complements, but you and the people around you use them every day. The following activities challenge you to find a connection between complements and the world around you. Do the activity below that suits your personality best, and then share your discoveries with your class. Have fun!

BUILDING BACKGROUND KNOWLEDGE

To Give or Not to Give?

If you've tried to write sentences with indirect objects, you know that not every verb takes an indirect object. Which ones do? Make a list of these verbs, and give the list to your classmates. Leave room for additions to the list.

FOREIGN LANGUAGES

The Order of the Day

How do other languages present subjects, verbs, and objects? In what order do they appear? What differences and similarities can you find between the sentence structures of English and those of, for instance, Spanish? Write a short essay detailing several of these points, or give a presentation to the class.

MUSIC

Beyond Firefighters and Cowboys

Do you remember when grown-ups used to ask you, "What do you want to be when you grow up?" Well, you're growing up now. Do you have an answer? Perhaps what you have is a lot of questions and a few dreams. Write a song about the problems of choosing a career. Include plenty of predicate nominatives and predicate adjectives. Then—you guessed it—sing your song to the class!

REPRESENTING

Four Branches, One Tree

Make a flowchart or decision tree that illustrates the process of identifying complements. Begin by noting the questions that you ask yourself at each step of the process. Transfer your chart to poster board. Use colors and other graphic techniques to help viewers understand your chart. With your teacher's permission, post your chart in the classroom where everyone can use it.

ART

Catch a Wave

Your classmates will remember direct objects better if you provide illustrations of specific situations. If you have access to a computer, page through the clip art and look for situations that may be described with direct objects. Print them out and make a collage, writing appropriate sentences under each one. If you prefer, cut out appropriate pictures from magazines and newspapers and assemble them into a poster. With your teacher's permission, hang your poster in the classroom.

WRITING

The Sincerest Form of Flattery

Do you have a saying or a sentence that you live by, one that you admire? Analyze the structure of that sentence. Identify its subject, verb, and other important elements. Then, taking that sentence as a model, write five more sentences that use that exact structure. You just might be surprised at what a fine writer you can be.

LINGUISTIC ANALYSIS

The Force Is with Him

Hey, *Star Wars* fans, have you ever noticed that Yoda talks rather strangely? Why is that? Check out a *Star Wars* book or listen to one of the DVDs, and write down some of Yoda's speeches. How did George Lucas make Yoda sound so special? What elements of the standard subject-verb-object order did Lucas invert or reverse? Begin by identifying the subject, verb, and object of each of Yoda's sentences. Then, identify the adverbs. Look out for the way Yoda uses *not*!

Literary Model: Poetry

Living Tendenderly

by May Swenson

My body a rounded stone
with a pattern of smooth seams.
My head a short snake,
retractive, projective.
My legs come out of their sleeves
or shrink within,
and so does my chin.
My eyelids are quick clamps

My back is my roof.
I am always at home.
I travel where my house walks.
It is a smooth stone.
It floats within the lake,
Or rests in the dust.
My flesh lives tenderly
inside its bone.

Exercise A Make a list of the predicate nominatives that appear in the poem. After each one, write the subject that the predicate nominative identifies. (Hint: In the first and third lines of the poem, the linking verb *is* is understood to follow the subject.)

Exercise B This poem is a riddle poem. Why is the use of predicate nominatives particularly effective in this type of poem?

Literary Model (continued)

EXERCISE C Using May Swenson's poem as a model, write a riddle poem. Use several predicate nominatives as you create clues for the riddle.

EXERCISE D

1. Make a list of the predicate nominatives that appear in your poem. After each one, write the subject that the predicate nominative identifies.

2. Swenson uses predicate nominatives to create metaphors. Are there any metaphors in your poem? If so, list and explain them below.

Writing Application: Report

Direct and indirect objects complete a sentence's meaning when transitive verbs are involved. Without them, meaning can be incomplete and even beyond understanding.

BEYOND UNDERSTANDING The emcee handed.
INCOMPLETE MEANING The emcee handed the award.
COMPLETE MEANING The emcee handed the glamorous actress the award.

Sometimes, of course, a sentence can do without an indirect object, as in this example: "The actress accepted the award with many thanks." Read each sentence aloud, listening for complete meaning.

Writing Activity

Every month or so, some awards show makes its way to television. Hollywood chooses the best of recent movies or people go online to vote for a favorite episode of a popular show. In "real life," too, awards ceremonies occur, from an elementary school awards assembly to the honors of graduation. Choose an awards ceremony, on television or in your area. Watch or attend it; then write a report for your school or local paper. Use direct and indirect objects as you list who won what.

PREWRITING First, choose the awards ceremony on which you will report. Then watch or attend it, but not as a passive observer. Take active and thorough notes of every announcement. Get a program from the ceremony, if possible; or you might be able to get information online. Gather all the data you can to use as you write your report.

WRITING Journalistic writing is brief, so write a sentence or two of introduction in which you tell readers the when, where, and why of the awards ceremony. Then list the awards, organizing them by category to avoid simply writing a list. Write a few sentences of concluding material, too, commenting on the interest or value of the ceremony.

REVISING You could write "The award for new artist went to Starla Lane," using a prepositional phrase to tell who got the award. However, since newspapers have strict space limitations, using object complements can make your writing more concise: "Starla Lane received the new artist award" or "The host gave Starla Lane the statuette."

PUBLISHING Check your report for errors in punctuation and spelling, especially capitalization of proper nouns and adjectives. Follow all instructions for submitting your report to the paper.

Extending Your Writing

This exercise could lead to a more developed writing project. For a speech class, investigate the appeal (or lack of it) of television awards shows. Interview people who like the shows, and talk also to some who dislike them. Consider why those little gold-plated statuettes grab the attention of so many people.

NAME CLASS DATE

Choices: Looking at Phrases

Here's your chance to step out of the grammar book and into the real world. You may not notice phrases, but you and the people around you use them every day. The following activities challenge you to find a connection between phrases and the world around you. Do the activity below that suits your personality best, and then share your discoveries with your class. Have fun.

FINDING EXAMPLES

Appreciating Appositives

Journalists like to use appositives because these phrases are informative and save space. Instead of writing an additional sentence, journalists often insert an appositive. Look through some newspapers or magazines, and cut out or copy examples of sentences that include an appositive. Paste your examples on poster board. With your teacher's permission, display them in the classroom.

VIEWING AND REPRESENTING

Mother Goos

Many nursery rhymes use prepositional phrases. Take a trip down memory lane, and read some Mother Goose nursery rhymes again. Find several examples of adjective prepositional phrases and adverb prepositional phrases, and copy them onto notecards. On the copies, underline each prepositional phrase and draw an arrow to the word or words it modifies. With your teacher's permission, display your notecards on your classroom wall.

HISTORY

To Be or Not to Be

Many famous quotations begin with or include an infinitive. How many can you remember? List as many as you can. Then, look through a dictionary of quotations. Pick several famous or interesting quotations that include infinitives. Write each quotation on a card. Include the author, date, and the work in which the quotation appears. Then, have your class vote on their favorite quotation.

MUSIC

Praising Phrases

Did you know music can contain phrases? If you are familiar with music, tell the class what a musical phrase is. If possible, provide the class with some examples. How can you tell where a musical phrase ends? Make a chart that compares musical phrases to grammatical phrases. With your teacher's permission, post your chart in the classroom.

DEMONSTRATION

Human Flashcards

Here is a demonstration that will help everybody in the class understand how adverb phrases can move around in a sentence. First, get together with a team. You will need several large cards. On each card, write an adverb phrase. Create other cards that contain the word or words each phrase modifies along with cards for the subjects, verbs, and complements of sentences. Each person on the team holds up a card and stands in correct sentence order in front of the class. Then, move the adverb phrase (the person holding the card) to different positions and read the resulting sentences. In addition, make a couple of adjective phrase cards, and demonstrate that these phrases usually cannot be moved.

ART

A Babbling Brook

Have you ever heard a brook talk too much? If you like a joke and like to draw, try this project. Illustrate participles that don't necessarily mean what they seem to say. For example, you could draw the expression *balanced meal* as a scale with food on either side. Display your images, but without the participles. Then, let your classmates write their guesses next to your pictures.

NAME ______________________ CLASS ______________ DATE ______________

for **CHAPTER 5: THE PHRASE** *pages 144–146*

Literary Model: Participles in Poetry

The 1st
By Lucille Clifton

What I remember about that day
is boxes stacked across the walk
and couch springs curling through the air
and drawers and tables balanced on the curb
and us, hollering,
leaping up and around
happy to have a playground;

nothing about the emptied rooms
nothing about the emptied family

EXERCISE A Write the two participles that are not part of a phrase. One is used twice. Then, write the four participial phrases and underline the participle found in each one.

Participles:

____

____

Participial phrases:

____

____

____

____

EXERCISE B

1. Which nouns in this poem are modified by participial phrases?

____

2. Which pronoun is modified by a participle and participial phrase?

____

EXERCISE C Using Lucille Clifton's poem as a model, write a short poem about an event from your childhood. Use several participles and participial phrases.

____

____

____

____

____

____

____

____

____

Literary Model (continued)

EXERCISE D

1. Rewrite your poem so that all participles and participial phrases are replaced with verbs or verb phrases.

2. Compare the use of verbs in your rewritten poem and the use of verbals in your original poem. Explain how the actions and events you describe seem different in the two poems.

Writing Application: Narrative

Participles and participial phrases allow writers to create a sense of action with modifiers. Present or past, participle or participial phrase, these modifiers pack a sentence with more interesting action.

EXAMPLE **Standing in the wings of the theater,** I fought my nervousness and waited for my cue. The leading man, **slightly distracted by the bright lights and murmuring audience,** stood next to me.

Writing Activity

As part of your training in a student leadership workshop, you are writing a narrative about a time when you faced an unnerving situation but eventually overcame your fear with action. You will present your narrative to the other students in a dramatic reading as the group investigates leadership qualities. Use at least five participial phrases as you describe the situation.

PREWRITING First, think about challenging circumstances in which you have recently found yourself. Choose one such circumstance, and brainstorm to recall all the details that you can. Use the *5W-How?* questions to think of information you need, and focus also on how you felt in that situation and how you overcame your hesitation and did what needed to be done.

WRITING As you organize your narrative, you can choose from several structures. For example, you could use a problem-solution structure, relating events as they unfolded in time, or you could try a flashback structure, starting in the present and casting back to an earlier time. Outline several structures, and then choose the most suspenseful and exciting one.

REVISING Stories tell well when they are descriptive and packed with verbals and action verbs. "Brown and furry, the bear's head was in the tent door" is not as interesting as "Slobbering and grunting, the bear shoved its head through the tent door." Use participial phrases as you would use vivid verbs—to create a sense of action and a sense of excitement.

PUBLISHING Check your narrative for errors in grammar, usage, punctuation, and spelling. You don't want errors to trip you up as you read aloud! Practice delivering your narrative dramatically to yourself and to a friend or family member. It may be that standing up and speaking before a group is a challenge for you—practice will make it less nerve-racking.

Extending Your Writing

This exercise could lead to a more developed writing project. Using your narrative as a springboard, create a fifteen-minute presentation discussing how people overcome their fears. Then, offer to give your presentation at a meeting of a youth organization or a teen support group.

Choices: Exploring Clauses

Here's your chance to step out of the grammar book and into the real world. You may not notice clauses, but you and the people around you use them every day. The following activities challenge you to find a connection between clauses and the world around you. Do the activity below that suits your personality best, and then share your discoveries with your class. Have fun!

CREATIVE WRITING

Mix and Match

Have you seen those sets of magnets that have a word or two written on each piece? By mixing and matching the words, anyone can create a catchy saying or a short poem. Think about the words that would be most useful, interesting, flexible, or funny in such a set. Then, make a set for the classroom. You can cut out strips from flat magnet sheets, which can be found at a craft supply store, and glue paper onto them. Be sure to include relative pronouns, subordinating conjunctions, and transitional expressions.

PERFORMANCE

Mad Scientists

Have you got a sense of humor? Well, here's your opportunity to use it. Write a skit about mad scientists dissecting a sentence. Naturally, you'll need to get white lab coats and create a special effect or two. Videotape or perform your skit in front of the class. During your video or performance, you'll be cutting up a sentence and identifying each of its parts. Since you'll be going to some trouble for this project, make the sentence you dissect one with several subordinate and independent clauses.

VISUAL

Subject to Approval

Finding the verb in a subordinate clause is fairly easy, but those subjects can sometimes blend into the scenery. Create a poster-sized illustration in which you highlight the subjects of at least five adjective clauses and at least five adverb clauses. Use color and other design elements to highlight the subject of each clause. Finally, with your teacher's permission, post your illustration to share with your classmates.

WRITING

In the Beginning

Some people have a hard time thinking of a story idea. Help your classmates get started. Think up twenty subordinate clauses with which to begin a story. Make some of them fantastic, such as "When strange flashing lights first appeared on that fateful day some twenty-odd years ago...." Make some of the clauses more ordinary, such as "Before Mr. Wiley and his five dogs moved in next door...." Type or neatly write your beginning clauses, and hand out copies to your classmates.

LITERATURE

If at First You Don't Succeed

Many an old proverb begins with a subordinating conjunction. How many of these proverbs can you remember? Working with a friend or two, write down as many as you can. Open your textbook to a list of subordinating conjunctions. It'll help jog your memory.

WRITING

If Wishes Were Horses

When you read tales of a person who made three foolish wishes, weren't you angry with the rotten choices that the character made? You could do better, couldn't you? Well, do so. With your teacher's permission, prepare strips of paper large enough for three sentences. Give everyone in the class a strip of paper. Write *I wish* . . . on the board, and tell everyone to write down three wishes, each expressed in a noun clause. Collect all the strips. Tape them together, write *Noun Clauses* at the top, and display the list in the classroom.

NAME CLASS DATE

Literary Model: Description

I can still remember the smell of the first girl I ever fell in love with when I was twelve. . . . Because I wanted to make a wondrous impression on this girl, grooming was suddenly important to me. Before puberty, happiness in appearance for me was pants that didn't fall down and a football that stayed pumped; but now I started taking three long baths a day and washing my own belt until it was white and shining my shoes until I could see in them a face that was ready for romance.

—from "The Only Girl in the World for Me" by Bill Cosby

EXERCISE A Underline the four adjective clauses and four adverb clauses that appear in this passage. [Hint: One of the adjective clauses is part of an adverb clause.]

EXERCISE B

1. Rewrite the passage so that it no longer includes any adjective or adverb clauses.

2. Without the subordinate clauses, does the paragraph sound different? How?

Literary Model (continued)

EXERCISE C Write a paragraph in which you describe an acquaintance. Use three adjective and three adverb clauses to help make your paragraph descriptive and to keep your style from being choppy. Underline each adverb clause once and each adjective clause twice.

EXERCISE D If you deleted all of the adjective clauses and adverb clauses in your paragraph, how would your paragraph be different?

Writing Application: Contract

Just as adjectives and adverbs can be used to make your writing more detailed and specific, adjective clauses and adverb clauses can, too. Your writing will be more interesting if you use subordinate clauses to vary your sentence patterns and to add descriptive details.

ADJECTIVE CLAUSE I bought the paint, **which was bright blue,** on sale.

ADVERB CLAUSE **When I dipped the brush into the paint;** several bristles fell out.

Writing Activity

Gone are the days when teddy bears, ducklings, or firetrucks decorated your room. Now it's even more *your* room, and you would like to personalize it. Your family, however, isn't sure about your plan to paint and decorate. To earn their support, draw up a contract in which you list what you would do to decorate and take care of your room. Use at least three adjective clauses and at least three adverb clauses as you detail your plans for your room.

PREWRITING First, imagine the perfect room—the room in which you'd like to study, sleep, and chat with friends. Describe it on paper; in fact, you could even draw it. List the changes you would need to make to bring your room closer to the ideal room you have imagined. Then, list the supplies that would be needed. You want to renovate as cheaply as possible!

WRITING A contract, even between family members, is a formal and serious document that clarifies expectations. Use formal language and a committed tone so that your family will sense your readiness to make your room your own distinct space. Like all writing, the contract requires organization. Write about what you will change in your room, then about what you will do to maintain your room. If you share your room with a sibling or two, work together on a plan that meets everyone's needs as fully as possible.

REVISING Sometimes writers are advised to avoid using first-person pronouns. In this case, however, first person is very appropriate. You are the one who will undertake the responsibilities listed in the contract, so make sure you have used *I, me, my, mine,* and *myself* where needed. Ask a friend or family member to read your draft and make suggestions to improve clarity or to make it more convincing.

PUBLISHING Check your contract for errors in grammar, usage, spelling, and punctuation. Mature, error-free writing is itself convincing! Give the final draft of the contract to your family, remaining open to suggestions they may make.

Extending Your Writing

This exercise could lead to a more developed writing project. For a class in art, you could check out research on rooms. What sorts of room shapes are comfortable? What effects do different paint colors have on a room's inhabitants? Investigate how interior environments influence our daily lives.

NAME CLASS DATE

Choices: Investigating Sentence Structure

Here's your chance to step out of the grammar book and into the real world. You may not always notice sentence structures, but you and the people around you use them every day. The following activities challenge you to find a connection between kinds of sentences and the world around you. Do the activity below that suits your personality best, and then share your discoveries with your class. Have fun!

CONTEST

The Long and Short of It

A simple sentence can be longer than a compound-complex sentence. Prove the point. Hold a contest to see who can write the longest simple sentence. With your teacher's permission, post the best entries in the hall where everyone can see them.

VISUAL

Lay It Out

For many people, nothing beats a diagram for understanding sentences. Prepare four sentence diagrams—one for each type of sentence structure. You may want to print the subjects and verbs in contrasting colors so that they stand out.

LOGIC

Common Denominators

All of the different sentence structures have some things in common, but each of the structures has its own unique features. What are these similarities and differences? Draw a Venn diagram or some other type of chart, and present it to the class.

LITERATURE

First Things First

Have you ever read a book or article that grabbed you with its very first sentence? How did that sentence do it? Find out. Identify the sentence structure of twenty different introductory sentences. Choose sentences from works that are special to you, to your friends, or to literary history. When you do your analysis, also note the purpose of each introductory sentence—is it declarative, imperative, interrogative, or exclamatory? Gather your findings together in a chart to post in the classroom.

PERSUASIVE WRITING

Madison Avenue Ace

Are you the sort of person who thinks that people don't understand the complex issues of our times? Or are you the sort who thinks the world would be a lot better if everybody just kept things simple? Use advertising to get what you want! Create an ad campaign for the type of sentence structure that best suits our times. Check with your teacher, and then post your ads throughout the classroom.

COMPARISON

Like a Pro

How do real writers use sentence structure in different situations? Get together with a group. Brainstorm several common speaking or writing situations, such as newscasts, editorials, and advertisements. Assign one of these situations to each group member, and have each member select and write down five sentences from his or her situation. (Reading articles and watching recordings of television are great ways to find material.) As a group, identify each sentence as *simple, compound, complex,* or *compound-complex.* Make a bar chart of your results, and discuss with the class reasons why your chart turned out the way it did.

ANALYSIS

How About You?

You've studied some of the world's great writers, but how do *you* use sentence structure? Look through your portfolio or journal. Pick out a few pieces of writing that are at least four paragraphs long. Then, count the types of sentence structures that you find. When you're finished, ask yourself, "Do I need to change my ways?"

Literary Model: Narration

The tall man stood at the edge of the porch. The roof sagged from the two rough posts which held it, almost closing the gap between his head and the rafters. The dim light from the cabin window cast long equal shadows from man and posts. A boy stood nearby shivering in the cold October wind. He ran his fingers back and forth over the broad crown of the head of a coon dog named Sounder.

—from *Sounder* by William H. Armstrong

The night passed, and the next day, after dinner, Redruth and I were afoot again and on the road. I said good-bye to Mother and the cove where I had lived since I was born, and the dear old "Admiral Benbow"—since he was repainted, no longer quite so dear. One of my last thoughts was of the captain, who had so often strode along the beach with his cocked hat, his sabre-cut cheek, and his old brass telescope. Next moment we had turned the corner and my home was out of sight.

—from *Treasure Island* by Robert Louis Stevenson

EXERCISE A In these two passages, underline each simple sentence once, underline each compound sentence twice, and circle each complex sentence. Then, complete the chart below by writing the number of times each kind of sentence appears in each passage.

	Simple	Compound	Complex
Sounder			
Treasure Island			

EXERCISE B Compare the styles of the two passages. What is the effect of including many compound and complex sentences? of including many simple sentences?

NAME CLASS DATE

Literary Model (continued)

EXERCISE C

1. Write a brief paragraph that might be the beginning of a short story about an event that took place at your house or apartment. Include both description and action. Try to use mostly simple sentences.

2. Rewrite your paragraph so that you use only compound and complex sentences.

EXERCISE D Which version of your paragraph do you think would appeal more to readers? Explain your answer.

Writing Application: Children's Story

Many fairy tales and stories written for children use choppy, short sentences—all in similar structures. Such writing may be appropriate for children, but it is not interesting enough for more mature readers. Avoid choppy writing by using the techniques you have learned to combine and vary sentence length and pattern.

CHOPPY The fiddler played his fiddle. His tabby cat suddenly began to dance. It danced on its front paws. The people shouted and clapped in astonishment.

REVISED When the fiddler played, his tabby cat suddenly began to dance. As it danced on its front paws, the people shouted and clapped in astonishment.

Writing Activity

Retell your favorite fairy tale or childhood story—first in short, simple sentences for an audience of little children and then in more varied, complex sentences for your own peers. Keep the events of the story the same; the only change should be in sentence variety and complexity.

PREWRITING Of all the stories you heard when you were a young child, which is your favorite? Outline the story—what are the events of the plot? Who are the characters? What is the conflict, and how is it resolved? If your memory lacks detail, head to the library to rediscover the story. Organize the events of the story chronologically, making sure to include the important particulars.

WRITING Retell the story you have chosen, first for an audience of young children. You may discover that it's harder to keep the story's energy going when you write in short, simple sentences! Using energetic verbs will help. When you finish the children's version of your story, use it as the basis for the more advanced version you will write next. Keeping your audience in mind, rewrite your story using sentence structure that appeals to students your own age. Write several versions of the sentences, trying out different sentence-combining techniques.

REVISING Read your two narratives aloud to a willing audience, making note of their responses and comments. Consider these comments for a day or two, and then prepare your final draft. When revising the children's draft, watch out for fragments. When revising the advanced version, make certain that you have not written any run-on sentences.

PUBLISHING Check both stories for errors in punctuation and spelling. Prepare both neatly. Then, work with a partner to create a children's book. Choose the story that you would most like to illustrate, and work together to design a book that combines words and pictures in an appealing, easy-to-read way.

Extending Your Writing

This exercise could lead to a more developed writing project. In a group of three or fewer, choose a fairy tale and find a creative new way to tell it. Perform the story as a modern-day drama, turn the tale into a comic book, describe the events in a news broadcast, illustrate the plot on a storyboard, or come up with your own format. Share your new fairy tale with the class.

Choices: Investigating Agreement

The following activities challenge you to find a connection between agreement and the world around you. Do the activity below that suits your personality best, and then share your discoveries with your class.

DISCUSSION

What If . . . ?

What happens when a pronoun-antecedent error slips by a writer or speaker? What if you were reading a cookbook that said, "Take one egg and beat them for one minute"? What would you do? Would you beat one egg or two? Prepare at least ten examples such as this. Then, discuss with your classmates the confusion (and ruined recipes) agreement errors can cause.

VISUAL

Peace and Harmony

What does the word *agreement* mean? What are its roots? What are synonyms for *agreement*? Make a list of these synonyms. Look them up in a dictionary. Think about the ways they differ. Then, design a chart like a wheel, with the word *agreement* at the hub. At the end of each spoke, place a synonym and its definition. Pass out copies to the class.

CONTEST

STOP!

Prepare a dialogue or monologue on audiotape or video. Sprinkle subject-verb agreement errors and pronoun-antecedent agreement errors throughout the script. Then, divide the class into two teams. Play your dialogue or monologue. When someone hears an error, he or she yells "STOP!" Stop and ask the person to correct the error. Proper corrections earn a point. Incorrect "stops" lose a point. The team with the most points wins, of course.

BUILDING BACKGROUND KNOWLEDGE

Rock-and-Roll

There are quite a number of pairs of nouns that go together, but actually name only one thing. These pairs even have a name—*binomial nouns*. Get together with a friend, and brainstorm a list of at least ten of these pairs. You could start with *macaroni and cheese* or *horse and carriage*. When you're done, pass out copies of your list for the class to insert in their English notebooks.

MATHEMATICS

Vital Statistics

Using measurements as subjects of sentences takes some getting used to. Give your classmates a chance to hear how measurements used as subjects sound with verbs. Choose a topic—the space shuttle, the *Enterprise*, or some other vehicle or structure. Write ten sentences that use measurements as subjects or antecedents. Remember to spell out numbers that begin sentences.

MUSIC

In Tune

Give a short oral explanation comparing the agreement of subjects and verbs to the tuning of a stringed instrument such as a guitar, violin, cello, or harp. If possible, bring your instrument to class and demonstrate how strings sound when they are in tune and agree. Then, demonstrate how they sound when they don't agree and are not in tune.

SURVEY

Guilty Parties

Polish your listening skills. Listen for subject-verb agreement errors around school, at home, with friends, and out shopping. Which subjects seem to cause the most problems? Let your classmates in on your findings, and give everybody a list of the guilty parties. No, not the people—pass out a list of the subjects!

Proofreading Application: Report

Good writers are generally good proofreaders. Readers tend to admire and trust writing that is error-free. Make sure that you correct all errors in grammar, usage, spelling, and punctuation in your writing. Your readers will have more confidence in your words if you have done your best to proofread carefully.

After all the work you have put into your writing, you want readers to be impressed by your work and to understand your message. Errors in agreement can make your work appear sloppy or careless and can confuse your readers. Careful proofreading will help you catch errors and ensure that you are presenting your best work to your audience.

Proofreading Activity

The following excerpt from a report on whales contains errors in subject-verb agreement. Find and correct the errors in subject-verb agreement in the following paragraphs. Use proofreading symbols such as those on page xiii to make your corrections.

Example Whales are fascinating animals. They are mammals, but they ~~lives~~ *live* underwater.

Unlike fish, whales does not have gills. Whales need air just like other mammals. They resurface periodically and breathes through a blowhole on top of their heads. If a whale get water in its lungs, it drown.

Whales are divided into two major groups. One group are the whalebone whales. Their name come from the bony plate embedded in their upper jaw, which are called a whalebone. They eats microscopic animals called plankton, which they strains from the water through their whalebones. Whalebone whales is large and slow. Blue whales, the largest animals of all time, belongs to this group. Other members of the group is right whales, rorqual whales, and gray whales. The second major group are the toothed whales. As their name imply, they have teeth instead of a whalebone. Rather than plankton, they eat fish and squid. This group include dolphins, porpoises, beaked whales, and narwhals.

Literary Model: Dialogue

Just the sound of the name brought Slade to my eye. . . .

"I don't think it's any good to send him a bill, Mr. Baumer," I said. "He can't even read."

"He could pay yet."

"He don't pay anybody," I said.

"I think he hate me," Mr. Baumer went on. "That is the thing. He hate me for coming not from this country. I come here, sixteen years old, and learn to read and write, and I make a business, and so I think he hate me."

"He hates everybody."

Mr. Baumer shook his head. "But not to pinch the nose. Not to call Dutchie."

The side door squeaked open, but it was only Colly Coleman coming in from a trip, so I said, "Excuse me, Mr. Baumer, but you shouldn't have trusted him in the first place."

"I know," he answered, looking at me with his misty eyes. "A man make mistakes. I think some do not trust him, so he will pay me because I do. . . ."

He took his pencil from behind the ear where he had put it and studied the point of it. "That Slade. He steal. . . . He sneak things from his load. A thief, he is. And too big for me."

—from "Bargain" by A. B. Guthrie

EXERCISE A In the passage above, underline each verb that does not agree in number with its subject.

EXERCISE B

1. With regard to subject-verb agreement, how does Mr. Baumer's speech contrast with that of the other character in this passage?

2. Why do you think the author has Mr. Baumer speak in such a manner?

Literary Model (continued)

EXERCISE C Write a dialogue between two characters, the first a person who has a certain mastery of English grammar and the second a person who is still perfecting his or her English-language skills. Have the second character use verbs that do not agree with their subjects.

EXERCISE D

1. In what ways was writing your dialogue challenging?

2. How does the second character's use of verbs that do not agree with their subjects help to characterize him or her?

NAME CLASS DATE

Writing Application: Report

Indefinite pronouns do not refer to a definite person, place, thing, or idea. They include words like *anybody, both, either*, and *everyone*. Some indefinite pronouns are singular, some are plural, and some can be either singular or plural depending on whether they refer to a singular or plural word. It is important to know whether an indefinite pronoun is singular or plural because the number of the pronoun determines the number of the verb it takes.

EXAMPLES Most of the play is set in the past.

Most of the characters are famous Americans in history.

The indefinite pronoun found in both the first and second sentences is singular when used with the singular noun *play* and plural when used with the plural noun *characters*.

Writing Activity

The editor of your school newspaper is planning a feature about the musical tastes of students in the different grades at your school. She has asked several students from each grade level to write a paragraph about the artists, CDs, songs, and types of music they and their friends like and dislike. Using indefinite pronouns like *everyone, nobody, many*, and *most*, tell what music you and your friends listen to and what music you can't stand. In your paragraph, include two sentences with singular indefinite pronouns as subjects, two sentences with plural indefinite pronouns as subjects, and two sentences with indefinite pronouns that can be either singular or plural as subjects.

PREWRITING Brainstorm with your friends to come up with a list of the artists, CDs, songs, and types of music you like and dislike. Depending on how long the list is, you may not be able to include every suggestion. Vote on which suggestions are most representative of your tastes.

WRITING Decide how to organize your paragraph. One possibility is to organize all your likes together and all your dislikes together. Another possibility is to organize all discussion about songs together, all discussion about CDs together, all discussion about artists together, and all discussion about types of music together.

REVISING Read your paragraph to your friends. Do they agree with your summary of the group's likes and dislikes? If not, what should you change, add, or omit?

PUBLISHING Check your summary for grammar, usage, spelling, and punctuation errors. Make sure that indefinite pronouns and verbs agree in number. Publish your report and present it to your classmates. If your class has a Web site, ask your teacher if you can post your report for students at your school to review. You might set up a page where students could post their own opinions about music.

Extending Your Writing

You may wish to develop your summary into a full-length article for your school newspaper. Instead of focusing on just what you and your friends like and dislike, conduct a survey to find out about the musical preferences at each grade level. Is there a diversity of tastes at your school, or do most of the students like the same kind of music?

Choices: Investigating Verbs in Action

Here's your chance to step out of the grammar book and into the real world. You may not notice verbs, but you and the people around you use them every day. The following activities challenge you to find a connection between verbs and the world around you. Do the activity below that suits your personality best, and then share your discoveries with your class. Have fun!

GAME SHOW

Trivia Trove

You are the host of a new game show! First, use a dictionary to look up ten words from your list of irregular verbs. You are looking for words that can be used as more than one part of speech. For instance, take the word *strike*. It can be used as a noun (*a* strike *in bowling*) or as a verb (strike *up the band*). During the game, you will ask questions such as "What verb describes the act of getting a band to start playing music?" and "This same word can be used as a noun in a game of bowling." Give a point to the first person who names your verb. If that person can name the past and past participle of the verb in question, the player scores an extra two points!

BUILDING BACKGROUND KNOWLEDGE

Limit: One to a Customer

Do your classmates a favor. Create a chart of all the verb tenses. For each tense, supply a verb and, if necessary, an appropriate helping verb. In order for this chart to be helpful, you must clearly label each tense. With your teacher's permission, pass out copies of your chart for everyone in your class to keep in his or her English notebook.

CREATIVE WRITING

The Family of Tenses

Write a short play for three unnamed characters who each represent a different generation within the same family. Each character will speak in only one tense—the past, the present, or the future. You might consider having the characters discuss technological advances. With your teacher's permission, perform your play for the class. Then, have your classmates vote on the family relationship of the characters. Discuss how the content of the dialogue and the verb tenses used affected the class's understanding of the characters.

INVENTIONS

Doodads

You are an inventor who has just designed a new household appliance or tool. Write a letter to potential investors telling them about the uses of this product and encouraging them to invest in its development. In your description of what the appliance does, you'll need to use vivid and convincing verbs. In your letter, you may want to include photographs or drawings of your invention.

TECHNOLOGY

Just Trust Me

Can you trust what a computer's grammar checker says? Put that software to the test. Type in a dozen or so sentences, all with errors of verb usage. Then, run the grammar checker. Keep careful records of each message that the program gives you. Record each suggestion offered. When you've finished, study the results of your test. What kind of errors did the program miss? What kind did it catch? With your teacher's approval, report your findings to the class.

ART

Show Me the Time

A series of illustrations may help show how each of the six tenses in English are used. Draw six different illustrations that each involve a single event. In your illustrations, give creative clues to the tense of each scene. Then, after you have completed your detailed illustrations, write a sentence beneath each illustration that describes the action in that scene. In each sentence, be sure to use the appropriate tense. When you have finished your project, put your creative and artistic abilities to the test. Tape a strip of paper over each of the sentences in your illustrations. Then, give the illustrations to a classmate to see if he or she can guess the tense in each scene.

Proofreading Application: Letter

Good writers are generally good proofreaders. Readers tend to admire and trust writing that is error-free. Make sure that you correct all errors in grammar, usage, spelling, and punctuation in your writing. Your readers will have more confidence in your words if you have done your best to proofread carefully.

People commonly make errors forming the past tense of verbs. Because most verbs are regular and form the past tense by adding *–ed* to the base form, it is easy to mistakenly apply that same rule to irregular verbs. The result is a usage error that can make a bad impression on a reader. The reader may think that the writer doesn't care enough to use the correct form or doesn't know what that form is.

In business letters and personal letters—especially letters to adults—be sure to use past-tense verbs correctly. Your reader will appreciate the effort you made to proofread your work and will think better of you for having made that effort.

Proofreading Activity

In the following letter, find and correct the errors in the use of past-tense verbs. Use proofreading symbols such as those on page xiii to make your corrections.

Dear Uncle David,

I heared that you have the chickenpox. I had the chickenpox once. It was awful! I itched all over. Everyone telled me, "Don't scratch!"

I had a busy week in school. In science, Mrs. Robertson teached us about photosynthesis. We learned that plants make their own food. In language arts, we readed "The Tell-Tale Heart" by Edgar Allan Poe. It was very scary! In social studies, we seed a filmstrip about Brazil. Afterward, we drawed a map of South America.

I bought you some books at the bookstore. If you like, I would be happy to bring them by your house. I remember how you lended me some books last year when I breaked my leg and was in the hospital. With your help, I also catched up on my schoolwork. I even maked better grades that semester!

Get well soon!

Sincerely,

Ben

Literary Model: Verb Tense

EXERCISE A By looking carefully at the verbs in Silverstein's poem, you can gather clues about when certain events occurred.

Jimmy Jet and His TV Set
by Shel Silverstein

I'll tell you the story of Jimmy Jet—
And you know what I tell you is true.
He loved to watch his TV set
Almost as much as you.

He watched all day, he watched all night
Till he grew pale and lean,
From *The Early Show* to *The Late Late Show*
And all the shows between.

He watched till his eyes were frozen wide,
And his bottom grew into his chair.
And his chin turned into a tuning dial,
And antennae grew out of his hair.

And his brains turned into TV tubes,
And his face to a TV screen.
And two knobs saying "VERT." and "HORIZ."
Grew where his ears had been.

And he grew a plug that looked like a tail
So we plugged in little Jim.
And now instead of him watching TV
We all sit around and watch him.

1. In the first stanza, identify one future tense verb and one past tense verb. Explain briefly why these two verbs have different tenses. (*Hint*: Remember that a contraction can include a verb.)

____

____

____

____

2. Re-read the second and third stanzas, paying special attention to the verbs. What is the tense of all the verbs in these two stanzas? Why do you think all the verbs in the second and third stanzas are in the same tense?

____

____

____

3. Identify the past perfect verb in the fourth stanza. Why is this verb in the past perfect tense, while all other verbs in the stanza are in the past tense?

____

____

EXERCISE B

1. In the poem's last stanza, identify one past tense verb and one present tense verb. Then, explain why these two verbs have different tenses.

____

____

Literary Model (continued)

2. In this final stanza, Shel Silverstein switches tenses in a clear and effective way. Are there any words in the last sentence that clue you in to the shift from past to present? Explain.

EXERCISE C Now it's your turn to tell a story. Write a story about an unusual or extraordinary event that either really happened to you or that you invent. You can write a poem or use regular paragraphs, but your story must include two tenses. Feel free to imitate the use of verb tense in "Jimmy Jet and His TV Set": Events that happened in the past influenced events that are happening now.

EXERCISE D Read over your story, paying special attention to the times when you switch from one tense to another. Do all of your tense shifts make sense? For example, you should not shift to the present tense while you are describing an event from the past. If any of your tense switches seem confusing or unclear, revise your sentences.

Writing Application: Narrative

One sure way to energize your writing is to avoid the passive voice and to use the active voice whenever possible. Lively active verbs can sweep readers along with your plot or argument, while ordinary passive verbs may lull them into a state of drowsiness. When you can, change the passive voice to the active voice.

PASSIVE VOICE The horses **were ridden** to the top of the cliff by the men in chaps and spurs. The train robbers **were being** relentlessly **chased** throughout the county.

ACTIVE VOICE Clad in chaps and spurs, the men **urged** the horses to the top of the cliff. Throughout the county, riders relentlessly **pursued** the train robbers.

Writing Activity

"Action!" yells the director as the cameras roll. Have you ever heard of a passive movie? That's doubtful, since *action* movies are blockbusters year after year. Many moviegoers want a plot that keeps them on the edge of their seats with thrills, chills, and spills. Readers often want the same effect, and writers can supply it by choosing colorful verbs and writing in the active voice. Try this experiment. Choose your favorite scene from an action movie. Narrate the action of this scene entirely in the passive voice, as in the first example above. Then, narrate the scene again, changing each use of the passive voice to the active voice and replacing any weak verbs with vivid, action-packed verbs.

PREWRITING You might try to rely solely on your memory as you jot down the scene you have chosen to narrate. However, memory can be spotty, even if you've seen the movie recently. View the scene in question again, several times if possible, writing down everything you see each time you watch it. You will probably catch something new on each viewing, increasing your appreciation of the movie.

WRITING Although the passive voice may creep into your writing now and then, you may find it challenging to use it in every sentence of your narrative. Use prepositional phrases with by and through to include the doers of the action, and be careful not to write run-ons, since passive voice can get a bit bulky. As you write your second narrative, in the active voice, change each of the passive constructions into active constructions.

REVISING Now that the narrative is in the active voice, read through it again, this time replacing any weak verbs with the snappiest verbs you can imagine (notice in the examples how *were ridden* becomes not *rode* but *urged*, a much more interesting and colorful verb). Consider replacing *be* verbs in particular, moving from state-of-being verbs to action verbs.

PUBLISHING Check both narratives for errors in grammar, usage, spelling, and punctuation. Watch especially for irregular past participle forms when you use the passive voice. Then, take both narratives to class, and read them aloud. After your classmates have read their narratives, discuss how the passive voice and the active voice affect readers differently. How does the use of the active voice affect the pace, directness, and liveliness of the narratives?

Extending Your Writing

This exercise could lead to a more developed writing project. As a research project, examine action movies. Why are people so drawn to action movies, even though they are not realistic? Interview people you know who are action-movie buffs, and do a little research on the Web. Then, present your ideas in an essay.

NAME ____________________ CLASS ____________ DATE ____________

Choices: Using Pronouns Correctly

Here's your chance to step out of the grammar book and into the real world. You may not notice pronouns, but you and the people around you use them every day. The following activities challenge you to find a connection between pronoun usage and the world around you. Do the activity below that suits your personality best, and then share your discoveries with your class. Have fun!

BUILDING BACKGROUND KNOWLEDGE

Pronoun Puzzler

Use a history book to research a well-known historical figure. Then, write four sentences that each contain the figure's name and an important fact about his or her contribution to history. In at least two of the sentences, try to use the figure's name as a direct or an indirect object. Then, remove the name of the historical figure from each sentence, and replace the name with an appropriate personal pronoun. Then, give your sentences to a classmate. Challenge him or her to identify the case of the pronouns you used and to figure out the name of your historical figure.

CONTEST

On Your Mark

The pronoun has many uses. For example, you can use a pronoun as a subject or as a predicate nominative. You can also use a pronoun as an object of a preposition, an indirect object, or a direct object. Write this list of pronoun uses on the board. Then, hold a contest. Put the class in groups. The first group to write a correct sentence for each of the pronoun uses listed on the board wins. You are in charge of the prize. Make it a good one!

HISTORY

Junkyard Blues

Whatever happened to those old-fashioned pronouns *thee* and *thou*? They wound up in the junkyard of English. Sometimes, good stuff can be found at a junkyard. You could make a poster titled "Junkyard of English." On it, write (or paste in fancy fonts) words and expressions that are no longer used. (Hint: To find archaic or obsolete expressions, look through literary works from other centuries.) Don't limit yourself to pronouns. If your teacher gives you permission, hang your poster in the classroom.

STUDY AIDS

Persistence of Memory

Invent a mnemonic device, or memory aid, to help your classmates remember which pronouns are nominative case and which ones are objective case. You could write and teach a rap or song, design and produce a sticker, or compose and teach a rhyme or sentence.

REAL LIFE

The Wall of Shame?

As a group project, make a bulletin board on which you and your peers can place newspaper clippings or magazine articles that contain errors in pronoun usage. Each clipping or article should be mounted on a sheet of paper with a written explanation of the error.

ART

Reflex Action

When a reflexive pronoun is used as a direct object, it directs the action of the verb back to its subject. For example, in the sentence "He hit himself," the reflexive pronoun is used as a direct object. Write three sentences that have reflexive pronouns as direct objects. Then, create a humorous drawing for each sentence to illustrate this ability of reflexive pronouns to direct the action back to a subject.

WRITING

Who's Telling This Story?

When telling a story, a writer typically uses one of two points of view: first person or third person. Use your textbook or a dictionary to research the meaning of each of these points of view. Then, write two versions of a simple story. Each version of your story should describe the action from a different point of view, either first person or third person. Highlight the personal pronouns you use in each version.

NAME ______________________ CLASS ______________ DATE ______________

Proofreading Application: Business Letter

Good writers are generally good proofreaders. Readers tend to admire and trust writing that is error-free. Make sure that you correct all errors in grammar, usage, spelling, and punctuation in your writing. Your readers will have more confidence in your words if you have done your best to proofread carefully.

Your reader's confidence is especially important when money is at stake. When you write a letter of complaint to a business, pay particular attention to proofreading for pronouns. Such letters often describe a series of events, and your reader may not understand what has happened if you have used incorrect pronouns. What's more, your reader may not take your complaint seriously if you have made such errors in usage.

Proofreading Activity

In each sentence in the following letter, find and correct the error in pronoun usage. Use proofreading symbols such as those on page xiii to make your corrections.

Example To ~~Who~~ *Whom* It May Concern:

My brother Eddie and me bought your Super Dooper Alien Robot for our younger brother and sister, who are four-year-old twins. Us children were horribly disappointed with your product.

To our shock, the big green alien yelled at my sister Lani and he and frightened them. Eddie grabbed the alien's nose; it came off right in his hand, so him dropped it on the floor. Suddenly, the nose hopped across the floor and squeaked; then little Uri jumped on it, slipped, and hurt hisself. Lani, whom had been crying, started laughing. To our relief, Uri, who the alien had frightened, soon joined her.

Even though the children did not really hurt theirselves, we want our money back. Please do not send we children another Super Dooper Alien Robot. Instead, make out a check to my brother and I in the amount of $29.89.

NAME ______ CLASS ______ DATE ______

Literary Model: Poetry

I Am of the Earth

by Anna Lee Walters

I am of the earth
She is my mother
She bore me with pride
She reared me with love
She cradled me each evening
She pushed the wind to make it sing
She built me a house of harmonious colors
She fed me the fruits of her fields
She rewarded me with memories of her smiles
She punished me with the passing of time
And at last, when I long to leave
She will embrace me for eternity

EXERCISE A Write the six different forms of personal pronouns that appear in the poem. After each pronoun, indicate whether the pronoun is in the nominative, objective, or possessive case.

______

______

______

______

______

______

EXERCISE B The personal pronoun *she* is used repeatedly as the subject of an action verb. *Me* is used repeatedly as either the direct object or indirect object of a verb. How does this use of personal pronouns support the central message of the poem?

______

______

______

______

Literary Model (continued)

EXERCISE C Using Anna Lee Walters' poem as a model, write a poem that describes your relationship with the earth. Be sure that your poem includes many personal pronouns.

EXERCISE D

1. Circle the personal pronouns you used in your poem. How does the use of personal pronouns support or add to the meaning of your poem? Did you repeat certain pronouns as Walters did? If so, why?

2. Do you think it would be effective to use so many personal pronouns in other forms of writing—for example, in book reports, essays, or business letters? Explain.

NAME CLASS DATE

Writing Application: Interview

In casual conversation, people often use the word *who* in place of *whom.* Though this informal usage may be appropriate in a conversation with friends, it is still important for you to know the difference between *who* and *whom.* In formal English—particularly in your writing—you should use *who* for subjects and predicate nominatives, *whom* for direct and indirect objects and objects of prepositions.

INFORMAL USAGE Who do you admire most?

FORMAL USAGE **Whom** do you admire most?

Writing Activity

Your history class has been discussing heroic figures past and present, but now the discussion has turned to "local heroes," those people whom you admire and want to be like in some way. To learn more about mentors and role models and the roles they play in people's lives, interview three people of different ages. Ask each person who his or her mentors and role models are and how they have influenced him or her. As you compile your interview questions, use *who*, *whom*, and *whose* formally.

PREWRITING Before interviewing someone, prepare yourself by deciding on a list of questions. Everyone is busy, so don't waste any of your gracious interviewee's time by showing up without questions. Brainstorm to create a list of five initial questions and two follow-up questions. Which questions will draw out the information you really need? Have you used interrogative pronouns correctly in each question? Set up and conduct three interviews with students in your class, teachers, parents, administrators, or others. Take notes of their responses as accurately as you can, or, with their permission, record the interviews.

WRITING Now you are ready to write up your findings in three paragraphs, one for each interviewee. Be sure to organize your paragraphs in one way or another—in order of your questions, for example. As you report the interviewees' responses, you will usually paraphrase their words, restating their ideas in your own words. Be certain that your words do not change the interviewees' ideas! Make sure you use the words *who*, *whom*, and *whose* at least one time each.

REVISING Although you will paraphrase most of the information you have gathered, you can make your writing interesting by including well-chosen quotations. Remember two points when you quote: First, you must give the quotations word for word—exactly as they were spoken. Second, you must use quotation marks correctly. Review their use if it has been a while since you last used them.

PUBLISHING Check each paragraph for errors in punctuation and spelling. Look especially for errors in the formal usage of who, whom, and whose. Then, write out the list of questions and the paragraphs—either on a computer or neatly by hand—in order to give your teacher a copy. Make a copy for yourself, and underline key points that you want to bring up in class discussion.

Extending Your Writing

This exercise could lead to a more extended writing project. Now that you have gathered information about role models and mentors, write a persuasive essay that suggests setting up or improving an active mentoring program at your school. When you combine your own experiences with those of your interviewees, you can write a strong argument about the importance of having role models.

NAME CLASS DATE

for CHAPTER 11: USING MODIFIERS CORRECTLY pages 265–280

Choices: Exploring Modifiers

Here's your chance to step out of the grammar book and into the real world. You may not notice modifiers, but you and the people around you use them every day. The following activities challenge you to find a connection between modifiers and the world around you. Do the activity below that suits your personality best, and then share your discoveries with your class. Have fun!

VIDEOGRAPHY

Go for Broke

Get together with a friend and test your classmates' ability to spot an incorrectly used modifier. Write a dialogue, just an ordinary everyday conversation. Fill the dialogue with double comparisons and other kinds of improperly used modifiers. Make your dialogue sound as natural as possible. Record your performance of the dialogue. Then, challenge your classmates tospot the incorrectly used modifiers. Have the class write down each error as the dialogue is played. The person who catches the most errors wins! Wins what? Well, that's up to you.

BUILDING BACKGROUND KNOWLEDGE

Wall Scrawl

Get yourself a big piece of paper and tape it to a wall or board. Then, grab a handful of colored markers and lead the class in a discussion of adverbs. Center the discussion on adverbs that might be used to describe the verb *write*. In fact, write the word *Write!* in big letters right in the middle of the paper. Invite your classmates to add whatever adverbs and graphics might be appropriate. When you're done, you'll have the beginnings of a great mural to hang on the wall.

MUSIC

Looking Good!

If you can rhyme, this is the project for you. You may want to pair up with a friend for this activity. Read over the rules for using modifiers in your textbook. Then, transform those guidelines into a song, rap, or chant with both rhythm and rhyme. Teach your song, rap, or chant to the class.

WORLD LANGUAGES

Over There

Do other languages have adjectives and adverbs? If so, how are these modifiers used? Do they appear before or after the words they modify? Do they have special endings? How do other languages express degrees of comparison? Research several word-for-word translations of appropriate sentences, and with your teacher's permission, write them on the chalkboard. Explain to your classmates the similarities and differences between the use of modifiers in English and in the other languages you researched.

TECHNOLOGY

Check It Out

Before you rely on a grammar checker, find out if it is dependable. Write ten sentences that use adjectives where adverbs should be used and ten sentences that use adverbs where adjectives should be used. Then, type the sentences and run a grammar checker. Record each change that the checker suggests. When it's done, tally the incorrect and correct changes and report back to the class.

VISUAL

Much More Than Many

Imagine that you are a top advertising executive. Your product, Giant Gizmo, offers much to the consumer. In fact, it offers more advantages than other products. Many features distinguish it from its competitors. Your job is to create a magazine advertisement that will make Giant Gizmo the top seller in the country. To do so, you will need to correctly use all the degrees of comparison for the irregular modifiers *good*, *much*, and *many*.

Proofreading Application: Scientific Journal Entry

Good writers are generally good proofreaders. Readers tend to admire and trust writing that is error-free. Make sure that you correct all errors in grammar, usage, spelling, and punctuation in your writing. Your readers will have more confidence in your words if you have done your best to proofread carefully.

Every year that you are in school, you will write more and more. Very likely, you are already required to have and write in at least one journal. You may even have two or three journals—one for science, English, history, and even mathematics. Some of these journals may be private; others will be read by your teacher and sometimes by your classmates. Writing these journals prepares you for a career. Scientists, for instance, must make regular and careful notes in their journals. Scientists, like many adults, work in teams. Journals enable teammates to understand the methods, criticisms, and results of experiments. Proofread this type of journal carefully to avoid errors that could confuse teammates and botch future experiments.

Proofreading Activity

Find and correct the errors in the use of modifiers. Use proofreading symbols such as those on page xiii to make your corrections.

Example To make a waterwheel, ^*we need* paper cups and plastic foam plates and tape ~~are needed~~.

The new design worked pretty good. In fact, it was the better of the three designs. However, the duct tape on the axle that was wrapped several times around was troublesome. The axle wobbled real bad and slowed down the whole process. Less duct tape and more better and careful application should be used on the next model.

I also suggest that we tilt the cups so that the water drains out more quicklier. To tilt the cups, a small bit of tape could be placed under the lip of each cup. Also, water comes out too slowly to turn the wheel from the hose. We just can't get no water pressure. Before performing the experiment again, the water pressure must be increased.

Literary Model: Using Modifiers in a Poem

A wondrous portal opened wide,
As if a cavern was suddenly hollowed;
And the Piper advanced and the chil-
dren followed,
And when all were in to the very last,
The door in the mountainside shut fast.
Did I say all? No! One was lame.
And could not dance the whole of
the way;
And in after years; if you would blame
His sadness, he was used to say,—
"It's dull in our town since my play-
mates left!
I can't forget that I'm bereft
Of all the pleasant sights they see,
Which the Piper also promised me.
For he led us, he said, to a joyous land,
Joining the town and just at hand,
Where waters gushed and fruit trees
grew.
And flowers put forth a fairer hue,
And everything was strange and new;
The sparrows were brighter than pea-
cocks here,
And their dogs outran our fallow deer,
And honeybees had lost their stings,
And horses were born with eagles'
wings;
And just as I became assured
My lame foot would be speedily cured,
The music stopped and I stood still,
And found myself outside the hill,
Left alone against my will,
To go now limping as before,
And never hear of that country more!

—from "The Pied Piper of Hamelin" by Robert Browning

EXERCISE A

1. List eight adjectives in the positive degree in the excerpt above. ____

2. List two adjectives in the comparative degree in the excerpt above. ____

3. List five adverbs in the excerpt above. ____

EXERCISE B Read the passage aloud, omitting the adjectives and adverbs. Then, compare the original passage to the one without modifiers. How are they different?

Literary Model (continued)

EXERCISE C Write a poem about a strange occurrence or a strange place. Use positive and comparative forms of adjectives and adverbs to describe the occurrence or place and to compare it to an ordinary one.

EXERCISE D How would your poem be different if you had used only positive forms—no comparative forms? Explain.

Writing Application: How-To Poster

"Lift the barbell with flexed muscles. Lowering the barbell, it is necessary to inhale slowly through the nose." These sentences sound a little funny because both have modifier problems. How can a barbell have muscles, flexed or otherwise? In the first sentence, the modifier *with flexed muscles* is clearly out of place. In the second sentence, who is lowering the barbell? The dangling modifier *lowering the barbell* has nothing to modify. Be sure that your modifiers are firmly tied to the words they modify.

REVISED With your muscles flexed, lift the barbell. Lowering the barbell, you should inhale slowly through the nose.

Writing Activity

Your school has just purchased new weight-lifting equipment, and students in gym class are compiling information on proper training techniques. Students will make posters with text and illustrations to guide their peers in weight-lifting exercises. Choose one exercise to describe for a poster, and write instructions for the exercise. Use at least four correctly placed modifiers to help students perform the exercise safely and effectively.

PREWRITING Here's an unusual prewriting technique: Since you are describing physical activity, perform that activity yourself and note what you do. Get your P.E. teacher to demonstrate the correct lifting technique so that you, too, will perform it safely. Notice what part of the exercise is hardest, what part tempts the lifter to cheat a little, and where your body feels the stress of the activity. Then, while the activity is fresh in your mind, describe it in writing.

WRITING You are writing a miniature how-to explanation, so a chronological organization is probably best. What do lifters do first, next, last? As with any how-to writing, point out potential mistakes so that readers can avoid them without ever having to make them. Use brief, clear sentences in your instructions; and since you are describing activity, use active voice.

REVISING The best test of a set of instructions is a trial run. Ask several friends to perform the exercise based on your instructions. Refine your instructions if your friends have trouble following them. Use correctly placed modifiers to clarify the instructions.

PUBLISHING Check your instructions for errors in punctuation and spelling. How embarrassing it would be if these were displayed on a poster board for all to see! Then, create the poster board drawings and instructions for posting in the weight room.

Extending Your Writing

This exercise could lead to a more developed writing project. Everyone knows that exercise helps the body. Beyond physical fitness, however, exercise brings other benefits. For the weight-room bulletin board, prepare an encouraging list of reasons to exercise beyond a healthy physique. Research these other reasons by interviewing health professionals and reading good books and Web sites.

NAME CLASS DATE

Choices: Exploring Usage

Here's your chance to step out of the grammar book and into the real world. Examples of standard English usage appear in your life every day. The following activities challenge you to find a connection between usage and the world around you. Do the activity below that suits your personality best, and then share your discoveries with your class. Have fun!

LITERATURE

Outlaws of the English Language

As the old saying goes, "You've got to break eggs if you want to make an omelet." Very likely, there are no great writers who have not, at one time or another, broken an established usage rule. However, they usually do so for good reason. Find some examples of this outlaw streak that runs through literature. Then, for each of your examples, write a few sentences that explain whether or not you think the author broke usage rules for an acceptable reason. Also, write a brief biographical note that provides a few interesting facts about one author. Be sure to include any important dates.

BRAINSTORMING

'Round Here

What usage errors are common among the students in your school and the people in your community? With your teacher's permission, get together with a group of friends and brainstorm a list of ten usage errors that are common in your community. Keep in mind that expressions that seem quite natural may be grammatically incorrect. If an expression is questionable, look it up in a usage dictionary. Then, make your own glossary of usage. Pass out copies to your classmates.

DISCUSSION

Beg to Differ

You've probably been speaking English for quite a while now, and you've spent a number of years in school. Surely you have an opinion about the usage errors listed in the glossary of your grammar text. Do any of these errors particularly annoy you when you come across them? Do any of the usage rules seem out-of-date to you? If so, which ones? After you've thought about these questions, list five of your least favorite usage rules. Then, ask permission to lead a discussion of them with the class.

ART

Picture This

Some errors are easy to see but hard to hear. Help everyone see these errors by illustrating two or three pairs of words from the glossary of usage. For instance, you could draw two cartoons illustrating the words *accept* and *except* or *bring* and *take*. With your teacher's permission, post your illustrations in the classroom.

WORD PROCESSING

If You Want Something Done Right

Some computer programs will automatically correct certain mistakes for you. However, you may not wish to rely too heavily on this feature. Investigate a program's automatic-correction feature. Identify the kinds of errors the feature can detect. Also, identify the times when this feature is appropriate and the times when it is best turned off. With your teacher's permission, present your findings to the class.

MEMORY DEVICE

Easy to Remember

Help your friends (or yourself) remember the solution to one or two troublesome usage problems. Write a rap, a riddle, or some other rhythmic lines. Then, teach your memory device to the class.

WRITING

Seen But Not Heard

Several usage errors are easier to see than they are to hear. After all, who can hear the difference between *alot* and *a lot*? Help your classmates see the difference. Begin by making a list of several errors that may not be easily heard. Write a sentence for each one. Your sentence should use each entry correctly. With your teacher's approval, make posters to hang in the classroom.

NAME CLASS DATE

Proofreading Application: Video Presentation

Good writers are generally good proofreaders. Readers tend to admire and trust writing that is error-free. Make sure that you correct all errors in grammar, usage, spelling, and punctuation in your writing. Your readers will have more confidence in your words if you have done your best to proofread carefully.

A video camera is ideal for certain projects: It allows you to communicate ideas that may be difficult to communicate through the written word alone. However, the fact that on a video your words will be heard—not read—does not mean that you should throw formal, standard usage out the window. Usage errors, even when heard on a video, can make a poor impression. Therefore, before you record a project, you should write down what you or others will say so that you can proofread for mistakes in usage.

Proofreading Activity

Find and correct the errors in formal, standard usage in the following introduction to a video presentation. Use proofreading symbols such as those on page xiii to make your corrections.

Example *You'll have to go a long ~~ways~~ way to find a better school.*

The Beel Middle School Ostriches welcome you to this here school! In this DVD, we're going to try and show you our school: the grounds, the building, the library, and the cafeteria. We have some real good teachers here. They can learn you a whole lot in no time at all. Our school it has some swell students, too; here are some right now. There ain't a school in the county with a better library than ours. We even have a awesome comic-book section; doesn't it look good? Here's the cafeteria; most students just make theirselves at home here. You won't find better food anywheres! We can't hardly wait to meet you!

NAME ______________________ CLASS ______________ DATE ______________

Literary Model: Nonfiction

In this excerpt, Jane Goodall describes her studies of chimpanzees.

As the weeks went by the chimpanzees became less and less afraid. . . .

On the eighth day of my watch David Graybeard [one of the chimpanzees] arrived again, together with Goliath, and the pair worked there for two hours. I could see much better: I observed how they scratched open the sealed-over passage entrances [of a termite mound] with a thumb or forefinger. I watched how they bit the ends off their tools when they became bent, or used the other end, or discarded them in favor of new ones. Goliath once moved at least fifteen yards from the heap to select a firm-looking piece of vine, and both males often picked three or four stems while they were collecting tools, and put the spares beside them on the ground until they wanted them.

Most exciting of all, on several occasions they picked small leafy twigs and prepared them for use by stripping off the leaves. This was the first recorded example of a wild animal not merely using an object as a tool, but actually modifying an object and thus showing the crude beginnings of toolmaking.

—from *In the Shadow of Man* by Jane Goodall

Exercise A

1. Does Jane Goodall apply the usage rule regarding the words *there, their*, and *they're*? List any examples of these words that appear in this excerpt. Then, explain whether or not Goodall used each of these words correctly.

____

____

____

2. Review the usage rule regarding the word *of*. Then, search Goodall's excerpt carefully to find the sentence in which she correctly demonstrates this rule. Write the sentence on the lines below.

____

____

3. Goodall understands the rule about avoiding the phrases *this here and that there*. Find the example of Goodall's correct use of this rule. Write the sentence on the lines below.

____

____

Literary Model (continued)

EXERCISE B

1. What one word best describes the tone, or overall sound, of this excerpt? Would the tone be different if the excerpt contained many instances of usage errors? Explain.

2. Why do you think it is important for Goodall and other researchers to avoid usage errors in their writing? Be specific.

EXERCISE C Pretend that you are a writer for a scientific journal, and describe in detail an interesting event you have observed—a family at the airport or a group of dogs playing at the park, for example. Your article should be at least two paragraphs long. Be sure your article includes at least five examples of correct usage, as outlined in the glossary of usage in your textbook.

EXERCISE D What one word best describes the tone of your article? How do you think your usage might affect your readers' reactions to what you wrote? Explain.

NAME ______________________ CLASS ______________ DATE ______________

Writing Application: Certificate

Read a typical diploma, professional license, or certification, and you will hear the most formal English imaginable:

TYPICAL DIPLOMA BethAnn Mistrot, having successfully completed the Course of Study as prescribed by the Faculty of the College, has been granted the Degree of Doctor of Veterinary Medicine and is entitled to all the rights and privileges appertaining to that Degree, in testimony whereof, the undersigned have subscribed their names and affixed the Seal of the University.

The great degree of formality speaks to Dr. Mistrot's accomplishments and the serious responsibilities that come with her degree. Writers seldom use such formal English, but when they do, it performs a useful service by calling our attention to and celebrating important occasions.

Writing Activity

How appropriate that National Teachers Day falls in May, as the school year comes to an end. Pretend that students at your school are preparing a special luncheon to thank teachers for their year of hard work. Your task is to write the text for certificates of appreciation to be given to each teacher. In formal English, write five lines of text to appear on the certificates.

PREWRITING Two prewriting exercises will prepare you for this task. First, find and read some awards and certificates that use formal English, such as that used in the above example. You could even check an etiquette source—book or Web site—to get a feel for this special style of writing. Second, brainstorm a list of the ways teachers help students. You may wish to cooperate with other students to generate ideas for the text of the certificate.

WRITING If you are worried about the formal language, don't let it block your writing. Instead, create the text first in less formal English. Write about fifteen sentences thanking and praising teachers. Then, choose the five sentences that best communicate students' appreciation. Make sure that your prewriting ideas show up in the sentences you choose. Finally, decide on the best order for the sentences. Often, certificates begin with the recipient's name, followed by a listing of the recipient's helpful activities and the name of the people or group presenting the award. Don't forget to include on the certificate the presentation date.

REVISING Now that you have the text in place, you can concentrate on formalizing the language. Refer to the glossary of usage in your textbook to make sure that the language of your certificate is formal and correct. You should also compare your text to the formal texts that you read during the prewriting stage. As you turn up the formal tone of your certificate, get feedback from other students and a few adults.

PUBLISHING Check your text—and let others check it, too—for errors in punctuation and spelling. Such errors would be embarrassing if printed up for all to see. After you have corrected errors in the text of the certificate, work with your classmates to produce a copy of the certificate to present to your teacher.

Extending Your Writing

This exercise could lead to a more developed writing project. In honor of National Teachers Day, you could write a profile of a teacher who has inspired you, for publication in the school or local paper.

NAME CLASS DATE

Choices: Exploring Capital Letters

Here's your chance to step out of the grammar book and into the real world. You may not notice capital letters, but you and the people around you use them every day. The following activities challenge you to find a connection between capitalization and the world around you. Do the activity below that suits your personality best, and then share your discoveries with your class. Have fun!

ETYMOLOGY

Check Up

Look up the word *capital* in a dictionary. From what language did this word originate? What are its roots and their meanings? How many meanings does *capital* have? Find the answers to these questions. Then, write a memo telling your classmates about your research. With your teacher's permission, share your findings with your class.

LISTING

My Hometown

For each capitalization rule in this chapter, find a real-life example from your town. Then, write each rule along with the corresponding hometown example. Ask for approval to post your work on a bulletin board.

RESEARCH

Winnie-the-Pooh

A. A. Milne, the author of the Winnie-the-Pooh series, often used old-style capitalization rules in which anything important might be capitalized. Investigate how he used capitals. Then, look for other works that use capitals in the old style. The writings of the U.S. Founders will be fruitful for this project. Make a poster that illustrates the old style, and ask to hang it in the classroom.

GRAPHIC DESIGN

Construction Supervisor

Prepare a capitalization exhibit. Include examples of modern poetry using few or no capitals. Modern art sometimes uses words with capital letters, so works such as Andy Warhol's famous soup cans would be good candidates, too. Computer programs, some of which are created in all capitals, would also be a great addition. What else can you add? When your exhibit is complete, ask for permission to display it in the classroom.

REAL LIFE

In the Diplomatic Corps

Find a good dictionary, and check out the variety of titles that people have all over the world. How are these titles capitalized? Make a list of them, paying particular attention to interesting ones as well as ones that you might actually have the need or opportunity to use in your life. With your teacher's approval, pass out copies of the list to your classmates.

HISTORY

Da Vinci to Picasso

Have you ever seen the fabulous, ancient paintings that decorate the walls of caves? We do not know the names of the artists who drew these masterpieces. We do, however, know the names of many other great artists. Who are they? Make a list of the world's great artists. Include at least one from every century since 1500. Include one from each continent of the world. For each artist, include his or her country, a brief biography, and the title of one famous painting. Post your notes (and illustrations, if possible) on a time line. Ask your history or art teacher to let you display your time line in his or her classroom.

GEOGRAPHY

Great Plains

How well do you know this country? Get a map of the good old *U S* of *A*. Choose a black-and-white map or make a black-and-white copy. Make a list of all the regional names that you have ever heard—Deep South, Midwest, and Great Plains, for instance. Then, get a U.S. geography book and learn about other regions. Use colored markers, paint, or pencils to outline or shade in each region. Use proper capitalization when you label each region. Hang your map in the classroom, or make copies for everyone in the class.

Proofreading Application: Letter

Good writers are generally good proofreaders. Readers tend to admire and trust writing that is error-free. Make sure that you correct all errors in grammar, usage, spelling, capitalization, and punctuation in your writing. Your readers will have more confidence in your words if you have done your best to proofread carefully.

Capitalization has many functions in writing: It announces the beginning of a sentence; it indicates a proper noun; and it is used in the salutation and closing of a letter.

Proofreading Activity

Find and correct the errors in capitalization. Use proofreading symbols in the chart on page xiii to make your corrections.

Example My Mother has always wanted to take a european vacation.

dear beth,

Today, we arrived in london. We flew out of John F. Kennedy airport in new york and landed at heathrow airport in london. We took the Underground, which is the name of the subway system, to our Hotel. After checking in, we were ready for some sightseeing.

First, we went to see buckingham palace, where queen elizabeth II lives. My sister, lisa, took my picture in front of its gates. Then, we visited westminster abbey. The english kings and queens have been crowned there since 1066! Afterward, we went to the tower of london, where the Crown Jewels are housed. We saw not only fabulous crowns, scepters, and swords, but golden saltcellars and spoons as well. By the time we were finished there, we were tired and went back to the Hotel.

We are resting up tonight for another busy day tomorrow. In the morning we are going to great russell street to visit the british museum. Then, in the afternoon we are going to the london zoo. I hear it has a wide variety of animals.

your friend,

Anne

NAME ______ CLASS ______ DATE ______

for **CHAPTER 13: CAPITAL LETTERS** *pages 308–322*

Literary Model: Capital Letters in a Fable

Long ago, the mice had a general council to consider what measures they could take to outwit their common enemy, the Cat. Some said this, and some said that; but at last a Young Mouse got up and said he had a proposal to make which he thought would meet the case. "You will all agree," said he, "that our chief danger consists in the sly and treacherous manner in which the enemy approaches us. Now, if we could receive some signal of her approach, we could easily escape from her. I venture, therefore, to propose that a small bell be procured and attached by a ribbon round the neck of the Cat. By this means we should always know when she was about and could easily retire while she was in the neighborhood."

This proposal met with general applause, until an Old Mouse got up and said, "That is all very well, but who is to bell the Cat?" The mice looked at one another and nobody spoke. Then the Old Mouse said:

"It is easy to propose impossible remedies."

—"Belling the Cat," retold by Joseph Jacobs

EXERCISE A

1. Write the words in the fable that do not follow standard conventions of capitalization.

______

______

______

2. Which standard conventions of capitalization were not followed?

______

EXERCISE B Why do you think the writer who retold this fable chose not to follow the standard convention of capitalization?

______

______

______

Literary Model (continued)

EXERCISE C A fable teaches a useful lesson, called a moral, about human behavior. The characters in a fable are usually animals. Create a short, original fable that includes animal characters. In it, use capitalization for effect, as Joseph Jacobs does in "Belling the Cat." The following list of morals may help you get started, or you can think of your own moral.

- It is best to prepare for the days of necessity.
- Do not trust flatterers.
- Be sure you can better your condition before you seek to change it.
- There are many who pretend to despise and belittle things beyond their reach.

EXERCISE D

1. What effect did you try to achieve with your use of capitalization? How would your fable read differently if you had not used capitalization the way you did?

2. In which other forms of writing might capitalization that does not follow standard conventions be effective? Explain your answer.

NAME CLASS DATE

Writing Application: Genealogy

Following the rules of capitalization will help you communicate clearly with the widest possible audience. When you write names and titles, you should be careful to write them correctly.

Writing Activity

Your social studies class is learning about genealogy, which is the study of family histories. Last week the class created charts with students' family trees. This week your teacher has asked you to write a short essay telling about three people in your family. You are to include at least the following information about each person: his or her full name, his or her birth date and birthplace, his or her occupation, and something special about him or her. Make sure to capitalize each person's full name properly. In your discussion, use a word showing a family relationship, such as *aunt* or *father*, in place of or as part of each person's name at least once. Also, at least once in your essay, use a possessive in front of a word showing a family relationship for each person.

PREWRITING Decide which three relatives you will discuss. Write down everything you know about each person. Look at your information, and make a list of what else you need to find out. If you can, visit or call the people you are writing about and interview them. If one of your subjects is no longer alive or lives far away, ask a parent or another relative about the person.

WRITING Try to do more than just list facts about your relatives. You are sketching a brief story of each person's life. Create a narrative with smooth transitions between topics. Feel free to include additional details to round out your portraits.

REVISING Have one of your parents or another relative review your essay. Are your facts accurate? Have you left out any important information about your family members?

PUBLISHING Check your essay for correct spelling and punctuation. Have you capitalized people's names and words showing family relationships accurately? With your teacher's approval, gather your essay and your classmates' essays into a booklet. Make a copy for each member of the class.

Extending Your Writing

You may wish to learn more about your family history. Perhaps you and a parent or grandparent could compile photographs of family members in an album and write short biographical sketches of each family member.

NAME CLASS DATE

Choices: Exploring Punctuation

Here's your chance to step out of the grammar book and into the real world. You may not notice punctuation marks, but you and the people around you use them every day. The following activities challenge you to find a connection between punctuation marks and the world around you. Do the activity below that suits your personality best, and then share your discoveries with your class. Have fun!

ETYMOLOGY

Detective Work

What does the word *comma* mean? What is its root word? Find out. Go to your school library, and ask the librarian for a dictionary and any reference books that explain the history of words. Then, prepare a handout for your class that gives the information that you have found.

ART

All in One

Get a piece of poster board and draw a giant comma on it. Inside the borders of the comma, write each comma rule and an example for each. You could use different colors for different rules. With your teacher's permission, display your poster in the classroom.

WRITING

Truth, Pure and Simple

Too many adjectives can be boring, especially when they always seem to come in the same place—before a noun. Show your classmates how to juggle adjectives. Write a poem in which you show the versatility of adjectives. Include adjectives before and after the nouns they modify. Use predicate adjectives as well. Be sure to have a series of adjectives that does not require commas and a series that does. With your teacher's approval, read the poem aloud to the class and post it on the bulletin board as a reference.

HISTORY

Once upon a Time

Pick an end mark. Then, find out how it began. When and where was it first used? Did it change over the years? Answer these questions. Then, prepare notes and illustrations to post on a time line. Be ready to explain your notes to the class.

STUDY AID

Rhyme Time

Devise a rhyme, rap, or some other kind of musical mnemonic (*mnemonic* means "memorizing") device to help your classmates remember the rules regarding colons. Write your own lyrics and melody. Enlist some of your classmates to help choreograph a routine for the presentation.

VISUAL ANALYSIS

Alike and Different

Why do we bother to have both commas and semicolons? What's the difference? Think about it. Make a chart with two columns: one labeled "Similarities" and the other labeled "Differences." Then, brainstorm ways in which commas and semicolons are alike and the ways in which they are different. Consider using sentences as examples. When you have finished your chart, copy your chart on poster board and ask for permission to place it where the class can read it.

ART

Around and Around They Go

Make a mobile or a wind chime of punctuation marks. You could use metal, ceramic, wood, or a mixture of media. Go ahead and add a word or two if you want. After you get approval from your teacher, hang your finished project in the classroom. Then, take a bow!

CREATIVE WRITING

A Checkered Past

Make up your own story about how semicolons came to be. Consider the following questions as you write your semicolon creation story. Why is their relationship to the comma not mentioned in their name? What is their relationship to the colon? Which do you think came first, the colon or the semicolon? Why?

NAME ______ CLASS ______ DATE ______

Proofreading Application: Written Announcement

Good writers are generally good proofreaders. Readers tend to admire and trust writing that is error-free. Make sure that you correct all errors in grammar, usage, spelling, and punctuation in your writing. Your readers will have more confidence in your words if you have done your best to proofread carefully.

No matter how carefully you choose your words, incorrect punctuation can confuse your readers. Punctuation conveys a lot of information beyond the basic meaning of the words in a sentence. For example, punctuation tells whether a sentence is a statement or a question, it shows how to separate words and phrases, and it indicates abbreviations.

Proofreading Activity

The following announcement contains errors in punctuation. Find the errors and correct them, using the proofreading symbols in the chart on page xiii to add or replace punctuation marks.

Example In order to raise the money needed for new equipment^ we need to hold a fund-raiser⊙

To: Soccer Team

From: Fund-raising Committee

We need your help The soccer team is holding a bake sale at the River City Mall on Saturday October 13, 2001 to raise money to buy new equipment. We need volunteers to bake bread brownies cookies muffins and other goodies. Of course we also need people to work at our sales table. There are three shifts available 1130 A.M. to 130 P.M. 130 P.M. to 330 P.M., and 330 P.M. to 530 P.M. If you are creative we could use your help on the advertising committee. Can you write draw or paint. Help us design posters! If you can help please see Mrs Adams. She is scheduling volunteers and she will also answer any questions you may have.

NAME ______________________ CLASS ______________ DATE ______________

for **CHAPTER 14: PUNCTUATION** *pages 332–354*

Literary Model: Punctuation in Poetry

in Just-
by E. E. Cummings

in Just-
spring   when the world is mud-
luscious the little
lame balloonman

whistles   far   and wee

and eddieandbill come
running from marbles and
piracies and it's
spring

when the world is puddle-wonderful

the queer
old balloonman whistles
far   and   wee
and bettyandisbel come dancing

from hop-scotch and jump-rope and

it's
spring
and
     the

          goat-footed

balloonMan   whistles
far
and
wee

EXERCISE A How do you think Cummings wants you to feel about spring? Use information from the poem to support your answers.

EXERCISE B

1. Rewrite this poem, adding end marks and commas and formatting it in a more traditional manner. You may want to delete one or two of the conjunctions that appear in the original poem.

2. Why do you think Cummings chose to write this poem the way he did instead of the way you rewrote it? Does Cummings' style—his untraditional approach to punctuation and formatting—help create the feeling you described in Exercise A? Explain.

Literary Model (continued)

EXERCISE C Using E. E. Cummings' poem as a model, write a poem about your favorite season of the year. To create a particular feeling about the season you choose, use little or no punctuation. Also, experiment with the formatting of the words on the page.

EXERCISE D How might the lack of punctuation and the nontraditional formatting of your poem affect how the reader feels about the season you chose?

Writing Application: Letter

Sometimes a writer interrupts a sentence with a nonessential expression that is used to modify an element in the sentence. This kind of expression is not part of the main idea of the sentence; it just provides the reader with a little more information. To show that an expression is an aside rather than part of the main sentence, a writer sets off nonessential expressions by using commas. A single comma is used with an expression at the end of a sentence. Two commas are used with an expression in the middle of a sentence.

INCORRECT I went to the movies with Becky who is my best friend.

CORRECT I went to the movies with Becky, who is my best friend.

INCORRECT *The Secret Garden* which was written by Frances Hodgson Burnett is my favorite book.

CORRECT *The Secret Garden*, which was written by Frances Hodgson Burnett, is my favorite book.

Notice how the meaning of the main part of each sentence would be the same if the clause were omitted. Each clause just provides some extra detail.

Writing Activity

Pretend that you are attending a summer camp on the moon. Write a letter telling your parents or a friend about the people you have met, the games you have played, the interesting sights you have seen, and anything else that would interest them. You may need to interrupt your narrative to add short explanations of who people are, how a particular game is played, or what a particular place looks like. Remember to set off these interruptions with commas. In your letter, use commas to set off at least six expressions that interrupt sentences.

PREWRITING Make a list of people you have met, places you have gone, and activities in which you have participated. Which items on your list will you need to clarify for your parents? Write down your explanations.

WRITING As you write your letter, decide where you will insert each of your explanations: at the beginning, the middle, or the end of each sentence. Where does it make the most sense to add the information? Where does it sound the most natural?

REVISING Let your parents or a classmate read the letter. Do they have any questions about who people are, what a certain game is, and so on? How could you add those details?

PUBLISHING Check your letter for errors in grammar, usage, spelling, and punctuation. Pay close attention to the use of commas with expressions that interrupt a sentence. After you have revised your letter, have some fun. Mail it and wait for a response.

Extending Your Writing

Consider using your letter as the basis of a science fiction story. Throughout the course of your story, develop interesting characters who face challenging conflicts. Be sure that your story has a beginning, middle, and end. As in your letter, you may need to insert short explanations about the people, places, or activities about which you are writing.

Choices: Examining Punctuation Marks

Here's your chance to step out of the grammar book and into the real world. You may not always notice punctuation, but examples of it appear in your life every day. The following activities challenge you to find a connection between pronouns and the world around you. Do the activity below that suits your personality best, and then share your discoveries with your class. Have fun!

FOREIGN LANGUAGES

The Case for Other Cases

Interview several people who can speak a foreign language, and ask them about the use of possessives in the language. How do these languages handle possessives? Do they have possessive cases? If so, do they have apostrophes? If a language does not have apostrophes, how does it indicate possession? Tell your classmates the answers.

CREATIVE WRITING

Time's a Wastin'

Writers can create characterization and tone in a story by using shortened words. By simply dropping the last *g* in a word like *going* and inserting an apostrophe, a writer can create a casual atmosphere and a more realistic dialogue. Try your hand at this skill. Write a dialogue that uses words shortened by apostrophes. Then, ask for volunteers to perform your dialogue.

INTERNET

:) or :(

Do you like to surf the World Wide Web or write e-mail? You can find some interesting punctuation in e-mail. Find out as much as you can about e-mail and the customs associated with it. Then, tell (and show) your classmates how punctuation marks are used in e-mail. For example, why is it considered bad *netiquette* (etiquette, or manners, associated with Internet use) to use all capital letters?

RESEARCH

Hy•phen•at|ed

Examine your dictionary to determine how it marks the best places to hyphenate a word. Does your dictionary mark where not to hyphenate a word? If so, how? Find out. Then, find five hyphenated words that appear in a printed source. Look up these words in your dictionary. Did your source print the words correctly? Tell your classmates what you learned.

OBSERVATION

She Said *That*!

You may have noticed that writers sometimes use italics for emphasis. Find a few examples, and read them (with emphasis, of course) to the class. Then, write several sentences of your own. Use your sentences to demonstrate to your classmates how italics may be used for emphasis. You should be able to move the italics around in your sentences as in the following examples: She *said* that! *She* said that! She said *that*! How does the meaning change when you move the italics? Report your observations to the class.

SURVEY

"The Secret of Life"

Ask each of your classmates to make up a title for a magazine article. The title should be special. It should be a title for an article that would be fun to write and would capture the readers' attention. When you have a title from each classmate, prepare a table of contents for a special magazine that you, yourself, will title. If you want, you can design a cover for the proposed magazine. Later, students can use your list to get ideas for essays.

STUDY AID

Memorization Made Easier

It takes some time to memorize which titles to italicize and which to place in quotation marks. Speed up the process. Do a bit of research on mnemonics. Then, write a few mnemonics to help your classmates remember what to do with which titles. Unveil your mnemonics in a presentation in which you also explain how mnemonics can be a great study aid.

Proofreading Application: Book Report

Good writers are generally good proofreaders. Readers tend to admire and trust writing that is error-free. Make sure that you correct all errors in grammar, usage, spelling, and punctuation in your writing. Your readers will have more confidence in your words if you have done your best to proofread carefully.

More than any other type of writing, book reports require the correct use of italics, quotation marks, and apostrophes. In book reports, you may also find yourself using other less common marks of punctuation such as hyphens, parentheses, and dashes.

When you are assigned a book report, you are invited to give and support your opinion of a book. Regardless of your opinion, be very sure that you proofread carefully.

Proofreading Activity

In each sentence below, find and correct the error in the use of italics, quotation marks, apostrophes, hyphens, parentheses, or dashes. Use proofreading symbols such as those on page xiii to make your corrections.

Example "No,^" I said, "I did not care for the book."

Lord Evan Poughkeepsie Smithfields *Autobiography of a Gentleman* is too detailed and too pointless to be worthwhile. This, his last work 1813, covers the period between Smithfields birth in 1752 and his retirement in 1807. In his famous essay Winter and Decay he views every tiny event in his life as monumental. For example, the author's descriptions of his breakfast foods toast, kippers, and finnan haddie are not necessary.

For a detailed list of the author's offenses, see Matthew Wellington's book of criticism Literature in My Day. Like Wellington, I grew weary of hearing over and over the words my dear reader. As Wellington so aptly puts it, "If Smithfield's readers were, in fact, dear, he would not address them so."

In conclusion, I heartily agree with Wellington, who recommends this book only to someone I would not wish this fate on anyone shipwrecked on a desert island. I make this recommendation, as Wellington says, "merely because the book is thick enough to serve as furniture.

NAME ______________________ CLASS ______________ DATE ______________

for **CHAPTER 15: PUNCTUATION II** pages 375–376

Literary Model: Dialogue

"You can't come in," he [the sick son] said. "You mustn't get what I have."
I [the father] went up to him and found him in exactly the position I had left him, white-faced, but with the tops of his cheeks flushed by the fever, staring still, as he had stared, at the foot of the bed. . . .
"Your temperature is all right," I said. "It's nothing to worry about."
"I don't worry," he said, "but I can't keep from thinking."
"Don't think," I said. "Just take it easy."
"I'm taking it easy," he said and looked straight ahead. . . .
I sat down and opened the <u>Pirate</u> book and commenced to read, but I could see he was not following, so I stopped.
"About what time do you think I'm going to die?" he asked.

—from "A Day's Wait" by Ernest Hemingway

EXERCISE A

1. Look back at the dialogue, and find the contractions. On the lines below, write each contraction that appears in the excerpt.

____

____

2. Read over the narration, and write the three clauses in which contractions could have been used but were not. (Do not include clauses from the characters' speech.)

____

____

____

EXERCISE B

1. What can you generalize about the use of contractions in this passage?

____

____

2. Why do you think the author chose to use contractions in this manner?

____

____

Literary Model (continued)

EXERCISE C Using this excerpt as a model, write a passage in which the narrator is also a character. Have the narrator talk to a child who is afraid. The passage should contain both narration and dialogue. Include many contractions in the characters' speech. Do not include any contractions in the narration.

EXERCISE D

1. Choose two of the sentences you wrote that contain contractions. Rewrite them, eliminating the contractions.

2. If you were to rewrite your passage so that it contained no contractions, how would the style of your passage change?

Writing Application: Analysis of Song Lyrics

Music can be silly or serious, but it is almost always meaningful. Songs can inspire us and show us a new way of looking at the world. Like poetry, the words to songs—called lyrics—have a special meaning to the author, as well as to those who listen to the song.

Like song titles, song lyrics show up in quotation marks when we use them in writing. When quoting a song's lyrics in your writing, be sure to put end marks in the right position when quotation marks end a sentence.

EXAMPLES Do you know the song that begins "Oh, how lovely is the evening"?
Yes, it's called "Campfire Song."
I'd like to learn the lyrics to "Strike Up the Band."

Writing Activity

While studying poetry in your English class, your teacher has asked you to write about the lyrics of a song that you like. (After all, lyrics are poems set to music.) Write a few paragraphs about these lyrics and the reasons that they stand out to you. In your writing, you will need to include some of the song's lyrics. Be sure to quote them accurately and punctuate them correctly. Then, play an excerpt of the song for your class, and share some of your observations.

PREWRITING Start by choosing a song: Look for one of your favorites (your song can be serious or funny) that you would feel comfortable sharing with the whole class. Read a copy of the lyrics section by section, and jot down notes about why you're drawn to the words.

WRITING First, make a list of reasons why the song you chose is important to you. You could tell about the first time you heard the song, explain whether your understanding of the song has changed over time, or describe how the music reinforces the lyrics' meaning. Outline your comments about the lyrics before you begin drafting. Be thinking about the best way to organize your paragraphs.

REVISING In a personal response to a favorite song, you will naturally want to use first person, and that's fine. There's no need, however, to say again and again "I think" or "I feel." Your classmates take for granted that your words are your thoughts and feelings. Also, when you quote lines from the poem in your writing, remember to keep the excerpts brief—a line here, a phrase there. A few carefully chosen words can carry the feeling of the poem into your paragraphs.

PUBLISHING Check your paragraphs for errors in punctuation and spelling, paying special attention to quotation marks. Then, decide how you will present your paragraphs to the class. For example, you could give your presentation using note cards that you've prepared or a poster that you've created. Practice your presentation a few times before taking it to class.

Extending Your Writing

This exercise could lead to a more developed writing project. Think of a play or animated movie that uses music in a powerful way. Choose one scene that effectively connects a certain song to the story's action, and write an essay about the scene. Include song lyrics in your writing, and explain how the song influenced the drama of the scene.

Choices: Exploring Spelling

Here's your chance to step out of the grammar book and into the real world. You may not notice spelling rules, but you and the people around you use them every day. The following activities challenge you to find a connection between spelling and the world around you. Do the activity below that suits your personality best, and then share your discoveries with your class. Have fun!

REAL LIFE

Bakers and Weavers

How did we get last names, anyway? We didn't always have them, so how did they come to be? What circumstances or events made them seem necessary? Research the history of surnames, and fill your classmates in on the story. While you're at it, find out what your own last name means. Investigate a few other surnames, too. With your teacher's permission, present your findings to the class.

LINGUISTICS

Pore, Poor, and *Pour*

The homonyms that you see in your textbook are not the only ones in English. What are some of the other homonyms that are often confused? Make an alphabetized list of at least fifteen of these word sets and their definitions. Be sure to make copies to hand out to your classmates.

REAL LIFE

Across the Pond

Have you ever noticed that some books spell *labor* and *color* with a *u* before the *r*? What's with these writers and editors? Don't they have dictionaries? Well, they do, but they are British dictionaries. British spelling and American spelling differ in several ways. Find out how and why. Then, give your classmates the lowdown.

HISTORY

Mass Production

Scholars say that the invention of the printing press greatly influenced spelling. Why on earth should they say so? Look in encyclopedias and history books, and find out. Mark any relevant dates on a time line. Then, use the time line as you explain to your class how and why the printing press influenced spelling.

INVENTION

Phydeau

What? You can't pronounce this word? It's a made-up spelling for the name *Fido*. Because English has borrowed so many words from other languages, spelling can be confusing. Take advantage of the situation! Invent new ways to spell at least ten words. Your inventions must follow an acknowledged pattern of spelling. Make a list of your new spellings, and see how many of your classmates can understand them.

GRAPHICS

Color Highlights

Some letter combinations tend to cause spelling problems. Survey your classmates or your teacher for the twenty most common spelling errors in your class. Then, make a poster of these words, spelled correctly, of course. Use a highlighter to emphasize the letter combinations that cause the most trouble. With your teacher's permission, hang your poster where everyone can see it.

STUDY AID

Day by Day

Take all of the entries in the words-often-confused list and use them to create a month-long vocabulary calendar. You'll need a piece of poster board on which to print or paste your typed entries. Some days will have more than one entry, especially if you want to take weekends off. Whenever possible, paste appropriate illustrations on the poster. With your teacher's permission, hang your poster in the classroom.

Proofreading Application: Public Notice

Good writers are generally good proofreaders. Readers tend to admire and trust writing that is error-free. Make sure that you correct all errors in grammar, usage, spelling, and punctuation in your writing. Your readers will have more confidence in your words if you have done your best to proofread carefully.

Errors in spelling are particularly embarrassing in public notices. In English, there are a number of words that are often confused with one another. These words sound alike but are spelled differently. When you write a public notice and misspell these words, they jump out at your readers. These misspelled words can make readers doubt the worth of your service, product, or event.

Proofreading Activity

Find and correct the errors in spelling in the following public notice. Use proofreading symbols such as those on page xiii to make your corrections.

Example Friends and ~~nieghbors~~ ^neighbors, do yourselves a favor.

Its that time again!

Spring-cleaning time is hear!

The days of cold whether are over.

Snow and sleet have all past us by.

Get you're car ready for those nice, warm spring days!

Better yet, let the student's of Niceville Middle School do it for you!

We're having a car wash from 9:00 A.M. too 3:00 P.M. on Saturday, March 1.

The cost is two dollares per car, three for trucks and vans.

Come to Big Ralph's Vegetable Stand at the corner of Central Avenue and Mississippi Street if you truely want to have the cleanest car in town!

Child care is available, and we have plenty of childrens' toys to amuse your young ones.

Literary Model: Spelling in a Poem

from "When the Frost Is on the Punkin"
by James Whitcomb Riley

The husky, rusty russel of the tossels of the corn,
And the raspin' of the tangled leaves, as golden as the morn;

. . . .

The strawstack in the medder, and the reaper in the shed;
The hosses in theyr stalls below—the clover overhead!—
O, it sets my hart a-clickin' like the tickin' of a clock,
When the frost is on the punkin and the fodder's in the shock!

Then your apples all is gethered, and the ones a feller keeps
Is poured around the celler floor in red and yeller heaps;

. . . .

I don't know how to tell it—but ef sich a thing could be
As the Angels wantin' boardin', and they'd call around on *me*—
I'd want to 'commodate 'em—all the whole indurin' flock—
When the frost is on the punkin and the fodder's in the shock!

EXERCISE A After reading the poem aloud, write at least ten words that the poet has spelled using nonstandard spelling conventions. (Hint: Do not include words in which an apostrophe indicates that a letter has been left out.)

______________________ ______________________

______________________ ______________________

______________________ ______________________

______________________ ______________________

______________________ ______________________

EXERCISE B

1. Rewrite lines 25 and 26 using standard spelling conventions.

____

____

Literary Model (continued)

2. Why do you think the author used nonstandard spelling conventions in the poem? Would the poem sound different if he hadn't? Explain your answers.

EXERCISE C ***Dialect*** is a form of speech belonging to a particular region or to a particular group of people. Think of a dialect you have heard in a movie, on television, or in real life. Write a paragraph spoken by someone who uses this dialect. Use nonstandard spelling conventions to help represent the dialect.

EXERCISE D

1. Will the nonstandard spelling conventions you used help your reader "hear" your speaker? Explain your answer.

2. In what types of writing would the use of nonstandard spelling conventions help you express what you want to express? In what types would it not help you? Explain your answers.

Writing Application: Definitions

Many sets of words in English are pronounced and spelled almost the same way, so it's easy to mix them up. When you're in doubt, look up the word in question in a dictionary or on a spelling list like the one in this chapter. Watch out especially for words that are new to your vocabulary. Otherwise, you may come up with embarrassing bloopers like these.

EXAMPLES I found the solution in *around about* way. (in a roundabout way)

The baseball player behaved like a *pre-madonna*. (like a prima donna)

The statues had survived for two centuries *in tacked*. (intact)

I am *a custom* to getting up early. (accustomed to)

Writing Activity

Your class is planning a spelling bee for fifth- and sixth-graders. These students may be younger than you, but they are a smart bunch, and you want to challenge them with words worthy of their knowledge. Each student in your class must choose seven words that writers frequently misspell. For each word, you must write your own definition. Then, write a sentence using the word correctly. (This sentence will be read to the student who must spell the word.) Finally, if you know any tips for remembering the correct spelling, write them down, too. Put each word on a 3×5 index card so that it can be shuffled with the other students' choices and drawn at random during the bee. You may use the spelling lists in this chapter or choose words that you have had trouble with in the past.

PREWRITING Prewriting for this assignment is straightforward: list the seven words you've chosen, and check the dictionary for exact definitions of each. Then, rewrite each definition in your own words. Be sure to note the part of speech for each word, too. *Effect*, for example, can be a noun or a verb, and its meaning depends on how you use it.

WRITING Now write your sentences to go with each word. The sentences should make the meaning of each word clear, and they should not challenge the spellers' comprehension—no trick questions. You may need to write several example sentences for each word so that you can then pick the clearest and most helpful example. Finally, attach to each word any tips you have identified to help remember how the word is spelled.

REVISING Enlist a couple of fifth and sixth graders who are not contestants to listen to your sentences (not to read them, since the contestants won't have that luxury, either). Which sentences most consistently prompt your listeners to spell the word correctly? Refine your sentences based on their feedback. Then, ask them not to leak any sensitive spelling bee secrets!

PUBLISHING Check your words and sentences for errors in grammar, usage, punctuation, and (of course) spelling. Then neatly prepare the 3 x 5 cards, and give them to the spelling bee reader.

Extending Your Writing

This exercise could lead to a more developed writing project. The spelling of words in English hasn't always been so fixed. In fact, not too long ago, writers had more liberty to spell words as they heard them. For a history class, do some research into how and when English spelling began to be regularized. You may be surprised at what you find. You may decide that you prefer the older methods of spelling words to our modern dictionary spellings!

Choices: Exploring Common Errors

Here's your chance to step out of the grammar book and into the real world. You may not notice them, but you and the people around you use grammar, usage, and mechanics every day. The following activities challenge you to find a connection between common errors and the world around you. Do the activity below that suits your personality best, and then share your discoveries with your class. Have fun!

PUBLISHING

Roll the Presses

Your classmates have created some great stuff for English class! Now it's time to form a committee to choose the best of the best and publish them in your class newsletter or on the class Web site. Assign someone to interview your teacher and get his or her opinion of the projects. Include a few photographs as well. When you have finished, you will have something really special to help you remember this exciting year.

DRAMA

What a Character!

You have probably noticed that errors in English usage are sometimes funny. Have you also noticed that certain errors can be used for characterization? For instance, you can use sentence fragments to characterize a scatterbrained person—someone who never finishes a thought. Write a brief comedy sketch. Include at least one character who makes as many language errors as possible. For contrast, have at least one character who never makes an error. Plot your sketch so that all of the characters are friends in the end. Select actors, and perform the sketch for the class.

MEMORY

Flashcards

Irregular verb forms can be tricky to remember. Help your classmates out by making a class set of flashcards. Choose several irregular verbs that have past and past participle forms that are hard to remember. Make a flashcard for each verb. On the front of each card, write the base form of your verb. On the back, write the past-tense form near the top edge of the card and the past participle form near the bottom edge. Then, test your classmates.

DISCUSSION

Pet Peeves

Just about everybody has an opinion about what the most horrible language error is. For some it's spelling, for others it's sentence fragments, and for still others it's incorrect pronoun references. Do you have a pet peeve? Do your classmates? Do your teachers? Find out by taking a survey of your classmates and teachers. Ask your parents, neighbors, and relatives, too. Then, use the results of your survey to lead a discussion on the errors that bug people the most.

WRITING

Who Says Friends Are All Alike?

Find out how different two friends (or three, four, or five friends) can be. Divide your class into groups of five or fewer, making sure that everyone has a pencil and a few sheets of paper. Have each group member write down the following sentence fragment: "before they went to dinner." Each person's job is to write a complete sentence by adding words to the beginning or end of the fragment. No consulting allowed! When everyone is finished, have each person read his or her sentence to the group. Repeat the exercise using a few fragments of your own.

ART

Fast, Faster, Fastest

If you like to draw or paint, you may be the best person to show your class how important modifiers can be. For example, when you draw a picture of three basketball players, you can make it easy for others to tell which player is tall, which one is taller, and which one is tallest. Now, pick your own set of modifiers and illustrate them. Make sure that your artwork has a caption that contains the modifiers you have brought to life.

Proofreading Application: Report

Good writers are generally good proofreaders. Readers tend to admire and trust writing that is error-free. Make sure that you correct all errors in grammar, usage, spelling, and punctuation in your writing. Your readers will have more confidence in your words if you have done your best to proofread carefully.

Many times in your school and work careers, you will be required to evaluate the writings of your peers. Whether your evaluation is graded or not, take care to proofread it carefully. If your evaluation is full of errors, your classmate will certainly not take your comments, criticisms, and suggestions seriously.

PROOFREADING ACTIVITY

Find and correct the errors in usage and mechanics. Use proofreading symbols such as those on page xiii to make your corrections.

Example This report fascinated me, but was difficult to read.

I knew that African Americans had influenced American music but I had not realized the importance of music in African life. The list of stringed instruments was helpful, but the lack of commas between items on the list confuse me. The instruments on this list was not familiar to me, so I wasn't sure if its names were one word or two. Take, for instance, the lute in the first paragraph that was mentioned. Was this a lute or a bow lute.

Moving on to the rest of the report. The section on african wind instruments was fascinating. The writer handled this material well, not an easy task for he or she. When all is said and done the biggest problem in this report was the spelling. I hope the author takes the time too proofread more carefully the next time.

Literary Model: Sentence Fragments in Haiku

The lightning flashes!
And slashing through the darkness,
A night-heron's screech.
—Bashō

A dragonfly!
The distant hills
Reflected in his eyes
—Issa

Broken and broken
again on the sea, the moon
so easily mends
—Chosu

EXERCISE A

1. Which of the three haiku contains only sentence fragments?

2. Which one contains only a complete sentence?

3. Which one contains a complete sentence and a sentence fragment?

EXERCISE B Haiku often try to evoke a particular moment or a particular sensation. Why might someone writing haiku choose to use sentence fragments?

NAME ______________________ CLASS ______________ DATE ______________

Literary Model (continued)

EXERCISE C Write three haiku on the lines below. Make each one three lines long. Some people write haiku with five syllables in the first line, seven syllables in the second line, and five syllables in the third line. Try writing at least one of your haiku that way.

EXERCISE D

1. Underline any fragments you used. What kinds of things, if any, did you use fragments to express? For instance, did you use them to express ideas, images, sensations, actions, or other things?

2. Underline twice any complete sentences you used. What kinds of things, if any, did you use sentences to express?

Writing Application: Dialogue

From now on, you will probably hear teachers warn you to avoid sentence fragments. These teachers are correct. Fragments should not appear in most writing contexts, so writers must know the difference between a fragment and a complete sentence. One writing context, however, demands that writers use fragments: dialogue. Speakers often use fragments—pausing, losing track of the sentence, backtracking, changing their minds—and always expecting listeners to keep up and fill in the gaps. Listen to your own speech and that of your friends, and you will hear many fragments, especially when a conversation gets heated.

EXAMPLES "Am not." "Are too!" "No way" "Bad dog!"

Writing Activity

In your drama class, you are exploring the special type of writing called script writing, the kind that is used in movies and television shows. For an exercise in how fragments can make dialogue more real, you will write two versions of a heated scene. First, write entirely in complete sentences; then, write in a mix of complete sentences and fragments. Other students will act out the roles in both versions of the scene. Then, the class will discuss which version works better in a script and why. The assigned scene involves a small group of friends watching a close game between two sports teams. Some of the friends are die-hard fans of one team, and the other friends have sworn loyalty to the opposing team.

PREWRITING First, decide on your particulars. How many friends are gathered around the television? What are their names? What sport are they watching? What teams are playing (real or fictional)? Who's cheering for which team? What's the score? Set the scene in which the dialogue will be played out, and give one of the characters a line that challenges the fans of the opposing team.

WRITING You're not creating an entire plot for this exercise, just a scene. Don't worry about coming up with the traditional beginning, middle, and end sequence of events. Instead, focus on who says what about the teams. Write the first version of your dialogue, the one that contains complete sentences.

REVISING Now put the dialogue you've just written in front of you and prepare to abridge it. When should you use fragments instead of complete sentences? The goal is to keep the dialogue's content *the same* while altering the way the content is expressed. Have a little fun with this version—"hear" these friends debating as you write. Then, identify each fragment you used by underlining it.

PUBLISHING Check your two dialogues for errors in punctuation and spelling—even a fragment should have good grammar otherwise. Then type your dialogues out or write them very neatly, so that your classmates can read them easily. In class, listen to the performances, and then discuss which version of each pair sounds more convincing, more true to life.

Extending Your Writing

This exercise could lead to a more extended writing project. Team loyalty is an interesting concept. For a sports class, explore the idea of life-long, or at least long-term, allegiance to a sports team. Interview some true fans, asking them why their teams mean so much to them. Talk also to a few avid sports fans who don't play favorites. What are the loyalists getting out of their teams? Are you yourself a fan (short for *fanatic*, of course) of a particular team or player? Present your research to the class, and see who's on your team and who's not.

Section 2: Practice with Sentences and Paragraphs

NAME ______________________ CLASS ______________ DATE ______________

for **CHAPTER 18: EXERCISE 1** ***page 455*** **PRACTICE A, WORKSHEET 1**

Identifying Sentence Fragments

DIRECTIONS Decide whether the following groups of words are sentence fragments or complete sentences.
- If the word group is a fragment, write *F* on the line provided.
- If it is a sentence, write *S*.

______ **1.** People and bears on the mountain trails in Glacier National Park.

______ **2.** A large number of grizzly bears in the park.

______ **3.** Park rangers teach people how to behave in bear country.

______ **4.** Want you to stay on the trails.

______ **5.** Should hike in groups of three or more.

______ **6.** Want to avoid contact with humans.

______ **7.** Grizzly bears when they see or hear humans.

______ **8.** Smart hikers make noise as they hike.

______ **9.** Talking, clapping their hands, wearing noisy bear bells.

______ **10.** To let bears know that they are there.

______ **11.** Mother bears with cubs are the most dangerous.

______ **12.** If you come across a grizzly bear on the trail.

______ **13.** People say you should not run.

______ **14.** Backing away slowly and leaving the area.

______ **15.** When you are camping in bear country.

______ **16.** Often not possible to climb a tree.

______ **17.** If people keep their campsites free of food smells.

______ **18.** Campers can hang their food supplies from a tree branch.

______ **19.** Cooking food away from the campsite.

______ **20.** If people use common sense when hiking or camping in bear country.

Identifying Sentence Fragments

DIRECTIONS Decide whether the following groups of words are sentence fragments or complete sentences.

- If the word group is a fragment, write *F* on the line provided.
- If the word group is a sentence, write *S*.

______ **1.** Amelia Earhart a famous American aviator.

______ **2.** Earhart was born in 1897 in Atchison, Kansas.

______ **3.** Was taught to fly an airplane by Neta Snook.

______ **4.** Setting an unofficial female pilots' altitude record.

______ **5.** Helped form an organization for women pilots called the Ninety-Nines.

______ **6.** The first woman to travel by air across the Atlantic Ocean.

______ **7.** Making Earhart famous.

______ **8.** Earhart married the famous book publisher George Putnam in 1931.

______ **9.** After a solo flight across the Atlantic in 1932.

______ **10.** Wanted to be the first woman to fly around the world.

______ **11.** Frederick Noonan was Earhart's navigator on this flight.

______ **12.** Their journey on May 20, 1937.

______ **13.** Earhart and Noonan took off from Oakland, California, flying east.

______ **14.** Landing in New Guinea on June 30, and leaving on July 1.

______ **15.** Earhart sent a radio message saying they were low on fuel.

______ **16.** Earhart and Noonan never heard from again.

______ **17.** A search mission for the missing pilots.

______ **18.** Although it is believed they crashed in the ocean.

______ **19.** Since no wreckage was ever found.

______ **20.** The disappearance of Earhart's plane a mystery.

Finding and Revising Fragments

DIRECTIONS Decide which of the following groups of words are sentence fragments.

- If the word group is a fragment, write *F.*
- Revise each fragment by (1) adding a subject, (2) adding a verb, or (3) attaching the fragment to a complete sentence. You may need to change the punctuation and capitalization, too.
- If the word group is already a complete sentence, write *S.*

EXAMPLE __F__ ^I was very unhappy When we missed the Watermelon Festival last year.

_____ **1.** We all arrived early this year.

_____ **2.** It was going to be a busy day.

_____ **3.** Chose the events.

_____ **4.** When my little brother won the watermelon-seed-spitting contest.

_____ **5.** My dad entered the watermelon-eating contest.

_____ **6.** After eating nine slices.

_____ **7.** My best friend was crowned Watermelon Festival Queen.

_____ **8.** My mom won third place in the watermelon toss.

_____ **9.** When she was awarded her prize.

_____ **10.** Was a volunteer at the dunking booth.

_____ **11.** Because I dunked him four times.

_____ **12.** When my mom said I couldn't ride on the Screamer.

_____ **13.** While I was on the Whirling Hurricane.

_____ **14.** Rocky Road and the Detours at the festival.

_____ **15.** Because they are my favorite band.

NAME ________________ CLASS ________________ DATE ________________

Finding and Revising Fragments

DIRECTIONS Decide which of the following groups of words are sentence fragments.

- If the word group is a fragment, write *F*.
- Revise each fragment by (1) adding a subject, (2) adding a verb, or (3) attaching the fragment to a complete sentence. You may need to change the punctuation and capitalization, too.
- If the word group is already a complete sentence, write *S*.

EXAMPLE __F__ After deciding to rent boats at the park, we were a little nervous.

______ 1. None of us had ever been kayaking before.

______ 2. A perfect day for a kayak trip down the North Fork River.

______ 3. The fall air crisp and cool.

______ 4. Falling from the trees along the banks.

______ 5. A lot of equipment, such as lifejackets, fishing rods, and picnic supplies.

______ 6. When we waded into the river to launch our kayaks.

______ 7. Rainbow trout eating bugs off the surface of the water.

______ 8. We found a good fishing spot.

______ 9. Took pictures of all the fish we caught before we let them go.

______ 10. Birds, squirrels, and even a snake.

______ 11. Because we were getting hungry.

______ 12. The sandwiches and salads.

______ 13. While getting back into my kayak.

______ 14. My splashing around made everyone laugh.

______ 15. By the time we reached the end of our trip.

Identifying and Revising Run-on Sentences

DIRECTIONS Some of the following groups of words are run-on sentences.

- Revise each run-on by (1) making it into two separate sentences or (2) using a comma and *and, but*, or *or.*
- If the word group is already correct, write C.

EXAMPLE ______ I have always wanted a motorcycle, and I'm saving up for one.

______ **1.** Riding a motorcycle can be a lot of fun it can also be very dangerous.

______ **2.** Motorcycles must share the road with cars and trucks these vehicles outweigh a motorcycle by several tons.

______ **3.** Motorcycle riders must watch out for other hazards as well.

______ **4.** Rain can make the surface of the road very slippery, loose gravel can cause a motorcyclist to lose control.

______ **5.** It's a good idea to take a course in motorcycle safety, courses are offered by many police departments and motorcycle riders' associations.

______ **6.** You'll learn the basics of operating a motorcycle, you'll learn how to react in emergency situations.

______ **7.** You'll also learn what kind of protective clothing you should wear when riding a motorcycle.

______ **8.** Many states require riders to protect their eyes, this protection keeps insects, stones, and dust out of the eyes.

______ **9.** You can wear motorcycle goggles, you can wear sunglasses.

______ **10.** The Motorcycle Safety Foundation recommends a full-face helmet they say it is the most important piece of safety equipment.

NAME ____________________ CLASS ____________ DATE ____________

Identifying and Revising Run-on Sentences

DIRECTIONS Some of the following groups of words are run-on sentences.

- Revise each run-on by (1) making it into two separate sentences or (2) using a comma and *and, but,* or *or.*
- If the group of words is already correct, write C.

EXAMPLE ______ Caves are hollow areas in the earth, part of the definition of a cave is that it is big enough to hold a person.

______ **1.** A cave can be just large enough for one person it can be as huge as an enormous room.

______ **2.** The largest known cave has 550 kilometers of passages, some think it has even more unexplored areas.

______ **3.** Limestone caves are common. They form when water dissolves the underground limestone.

______ **4.** Water remains in some caves, it forms deep underground lakes.

______ **5.** One type of cave is formed when underground lava cools first on the outside the molten lava inside then exits, leaving a hollow place.

______ **6.** Crashing surf makes "sea caves," the water breaks down rock along the shore.

______ **7.** A sinkhole is a cave with its entrance in the "roof," have you ever stumbled upon a sinkhole?

______ **8.** Stalactites and stalagmites are cave formations made from minerals deposited by dripping water.

______ **9.** Stalactites hang from the ceiling of a cave, stalagmites rise from its floor.

______ **10.** These cave formations look like icicles and pillars individually, they form a column from floor to ceiling when they connect.

Correcting Sentence Fragments and Run-ons

DIRECTIONS The following paragraph contains several sentence fragments and run-on sentences.

- Underline the sentence fragments once and the run-on sentences twice.
- Rewrite the paragraph to eliminate the sentence fragments and correct the run-on sentences.
- Change the punctuation and capitalization as necessary to make each sentence clear and complete.

The human brain is made up of three main parts the three parts work together to carry out complicated tasks. The cerebrum is where information from your senses is processed. When your eyes see a skunk in the road. Your cerebrum tells your arms to move the steering wheel to avoid it. The cerebellum controls balance and coordination, this is the part of the brain that helps you hold a soft drink and change the radio station at the same time. When you almost have a head-on collision from trying to do too many things at once. The brain stem brings your heart rate back to normal.

NAME CLASS DATE

for **CHAPTER 18: REVIEW A** *page 458* **PRACTICE B, WORKSHEET 8**

Correcting Sentence Fragments and Run-ons

DIRECTIONS The following paragraph contains several sentence fragments and run-on sentences.

- Underline the sentence fragments once and the run-on sentences twice.
- Rewrite the paragraph to eliminate the sentence fragments and correct the run-on sentences.
- Change the punctuation and capitalization as necessary to make each sentence clear and complete.

The ancient Egyptians preserved the bodies of the dead with a special process of embalming the entire process took about seventy days. One of the first steps was removing the internal organs. Most of the organs taken out and placed in jars. A kind of rock salt was then used to dry the body. Once the body had dried completely. The Egyptians filled it with material to preserve its shape. Different materials were used. They packed the body with linen pads they filled it with sawdust. Next, the body was wrapped in many layers of linen bandages. When the wrapping was completed. The mummy was placed in a coffin. The ancient Egyptians' process very effective. Scientists sometimes unwrap mummies to study them. The bodies have deteriorated, you can still tell what the person looked like when he or she was alive.

Combining Sentences by Inserting Words

DIRECTIONS Each of the following items contains two sentences. To combine the two sentences, take the italicized key word from the second sentence and insert it into the first sentence. The directions in parentheses will tell you how to change the form of the key word if needed.

1. A horse is born ready to stand on its own legs. It has *four* legs.

2. However, a kangaroo is born developed. Its development is *partial*. (Add *-ly*.)

3. A newborn kangaroo must climb into its mother's pouch. The pouch is *warm*.

4. The baby kangaroo grows in the pouch. The kangaroo grows *slowly*.

5. The kangaroo will have large hind legs as an adult. Its legs will have a lot of *power*. (Add *-ful*.)

6. Kangaroos use their hind legs to hop at speeds up to thirty miles per hour. They use the *strength* of their hind legs. (Change *strength* to *strong*.)

7. A kangaroo uses its tail for support and balance. It has a *long* tail.

8. Kangaroos' ears can twist forward and backward. They *use* their ears constantly. (Add *-ful*.)

9. Kangaroos are preyed upon by dogs called dingoes. These dogs live in *Australia*. (Change *Australia* to *Australian*.)

10. Laws protect kangaroos from human hunters. These laws are *strict*.

NAME ______________________ CLASS ______________ DATE ______________

for **CHAPTER 18: EXERCISE 4** *page 460* **PRACTICE B, WORKSHEET 10**

Combining Sentences by Inserting Words

DIRECTIONS Each of the following items contains two sentences. To combine the two sentences, take the italicized key word from the second sentence and insert it into the first sentence. The directions in parentheses will tell you how to change the form of the key word if needed.

1. Sleep is a state shared by human beings and animals. Sleep is *important*.

____

2. Scientists study people's habits. They study their habits when they *sleep*. (Add *-ing*.)

____

3. A sensitive machine can show how the brain functions during sleep. The machine's sensitivity is *high*. (Add *-ly*.)

____

4. Waking people's brains give off about ten electrical waves per second. The waves are *small*.

____

5. Brain waves continue during sleep. The brain waves *vary*. (Add *-ing*.)

____

6. People need both slow-moving and fast-moving brain waves for sleep. The sleep helps people *rest*. (Add *-ful*.)

____

7. People have eye movements when they experience fast-moving brain waves. The eye movements are *rapid*.

____

____

8. Dreams occur during REM (rapid eye movement) sleep. The dreams are *vivid*.

____

9. People sometimes question what their dreams mean. Their dreams *puzzle* them. (Add *-ing*.)

____

10. People who are prevented from entering deep sleep become irritable. It is an *eventual* result of missing deep sleep. (Add *-ly*.)

____

____

NAME ____________ CLASS ____________ DATE ____________

for **CHAPTER 18: EXERCISE 5** *page 462* **PRACTICE A, WORKSHEET 11**

Combining Sentences by Inserting Phrases

DIRECTIONS Each of the following items contains two sentences. To combine the sentences, take the italicized word group from the second sentence and insert it into the first sentence. The hints in parentheses will tell you how to change the forms of words if needed.

1. Travelers can cross the United States in a matter of hours. They can do this *by airplane.*

2. The eight-thousand-mile journey of Meriwether Lewis and William Clark was no vacation. They were *the leaders of the Lewis and Clark expedition.*

3. President Thomas Jefferson sent a team of explorers westward. He *hoped to establish a route to the Pacific coast.* (Change *hoped* to *hoping.*)

4. In 1804, the group led by Lewis and Clark set out from St. Louis on its journey. It was *to explore the northwestern region.*

5. The explorers had problems from the very beginning of the journey. They *had to paddle their heavy boats upstream against the swift current of the Missouri River.* (Change *had* to *having.*)

6. The explorers tried to establish good relations with the Native Americans they met. They *gave them presents.* (Change *gave* to *by giving.*)

7. Many people the explorers met were friendly. They were *eager to offer food and advice.*

8. Sacagawea joined the expedition team as an interpreter. She was *a Shoshone woman.*

9. The team began a very difficult part of its journey. They *crossed the Bitterroot Mountains.* (Change *crossed* to *after crossing.*)

10. When they reached the Pacific Ocean, they built a fort where they spent the winter. There they *gathered strength for their long trip home.* (Change *gathered* to *gathering.*)

Combining Sentences by Inserting Phrases

DIRECTIONS Each of the following items contains two sentences. To combine the sentences, take the italicized word group from the second sentence and insert it into the first sentence. The hints in parentheses will tell you how to change the forms of words if needed.

1. Many animals migrate from the place where they were born. They migrate *to find food or better living conditions.*

2. Some animals make one great journey in their lifetime. They are *like the Pacific salmon.*

3. Salmon are born in freshwater streams but live most of their adult lives in the ocean. They *return upstream to spawn.* (Change *return* to *returning.*)

4. After spawning, the Pacific salmon dies. It *has completed its life cycle.* (Change *has completed* to *having completed.*)

5. Other animals migrate annually. They *make a round-trip journey.* (Change *make* to *making.*)

6. Some birds go south for the winter. They *sense the change of seasons.* (Change *sense* to *sensing.*)

7. Scientists believe that a bird's "inner calendar" tells it when to return home in the spring. The inner calendar is *present at birth.*

8. The arctic tern is one of the record holders for long-distance migrations. It *travels up to 22,000 miles in a year.* (Change *travels* to *traveling.*)

9. Adult humpback whales spend most of their time where their food supply is most abundant. They live *in the icy water of the polar regions.*

10. When a female whale is ready to give birth, she and her mate migrate to warmer tropical waters. They migrate *for the sake of the newborn calf.*

Creating Compound Subjects and Verbs

DIRECTIONS Combine each of the following pairs of short, choppy sentences by using *and, but,* or *or.*

- If the two sentences have the same verb, make a compound subject.
- If they have the same subject, make a compound verb.

1. Toads belong to a group of animals called amphibians. Frogs belong to a group of animals called amphibians.

2. They can survive in water. They can survive on land.

3. Female toads can lay thousands of eggs at a time. Female frogs can lay thousands of eggs at a time.

4. Tadpoles hatch from the eggs. Tadpoles remain in the water as they mature into adult frogs.

5. Toads do not like direct sunlight. Toads are most active during rainy days or at night.

6. People cannot get warts from touching toads. People can get sick from touching poisonous glands on a toad's head.

7. Toads burrow to escape extreme weather. Toads hibernate to escape extreme weather.

8. Frogs are beneficial to humans because they eat insect pests. Toads are beneficial to humans for the same reason.

9. The cane toad is one of the largest toads. The cane toad can grow up to nine inches in length.

10. The Goliath frog of West Africa is the largest frog. The Goliath frog weighs about seven pounds.

Creating Compound Subjects and Verbs

DIRECTIONS Combine each of the following pairs of short, choppy sentences by using *and, but,* or *or.*

- If the two sentences have the same verb, make a compound subject.
- If they have the same subject, make a compound verb.

1. Alligators are reptiles. Crocodiles are reptiles.

2. Both animals' eyes sit high on their heads. Both animals' eyes let them see above water.

3. Crocodiles use their short, strong legs for walking on land. Crocodiles swim by moving their tails from side to side.

4. A crocodile looks much like an alligator. A crocodile weighs only about two-thirds as much as an alligator.

5. Crocodiles eat small animals such as fish and birds. Crocodiles occasionally attack large animals and people.

6. Alligators have long snouts and sharp teeth. Crocodiles have long snouts and sharp teeth.

7. An alligator's snout is long. An alligator's snout is broader and more rounded than a crocodile's snout.

8. Crocodiles hide their eggs in nests of brush or leaves. Crocodiles bury their eggs in the sand.

9. Crocodiles were once widely hunted for their hides. Alligators were once widely hunted for their hides.

10. Alligators were once classified as an endangered species. Alligators have been reclassified because their numbers are increasing.

Forming Compound Sentences

DIRECTIONS Each of the following pairs of sentences is closely related. Make each pair a compound sentence by adding a comma and a coordinating conjunction such as *and* or *but*.

EXAMPLE The Sahara is almost as big as the United States, but it has only two million inhabitants.

1. This desert has one of the world's harshest climates. Large portions of it are completely uninhabited.
2. The word *Sahara* comes from the Arabic word for desert. Different parts of this desert have other names.
3. The Sahara contains valuable minerals such as copper, iron, tin, and gold. Many of these have not yet been mined.
4. The Saharan climate is hot and dry. The air turns cool at night.
5. Much of the desert consists of vast seas of sand called *ergs*. The shifting sand in these ergs can form dunes as high as 600 feet.
6. The landscape of the Sahara does not change for mile after mile. This is probably why it is nicknamed "ocean of the sands."
7. People believe that a continuous sandy landscape is typical of the Sahara. This terrain accounts for only one-eighth of the desert's area.
8. The Painted Desert in Arizona differs in character from the Sahara. Its name indicates its more colorful terrain.
9. Its brightly colored rocks impressed a U.S. government explorer. He chose the name "painted" to describe the place.
10. Navajo and Hopi reservations are part of the Painted Desert. The Navajo use the colorful sands to make ceremonial paintings.

Forming Compound Sentences

DIRECTIONS Each of the following pairs of sentences is closely related. Make each pair a compound sentence by adding a comma and a coordinating conjunction such as *and* or *but*.

EXAMPLE Pompeii was an ancient city in Italy, and it was buried under the ashes of a volcanic eruption in A.D. 79.

1. Earthquakes damaged the ancient city in A.D. 62. It was a volcanic eruption that ultimately destroyed Pompeii.

2. Pompeii was not famous in its time. It is better known today because its ruins are so well preserved.

3. Mount Vesuvius erupted violently in the summer of A.D. 79. Pompeii was engulfed in hot ashes and poisonous gases.

4. When the ashes fell on Pompeii, much of the city was buried. Only columns and rooftops were left visible.

5. Survivors recovered some valuables that they had left behind in the city. Later eruptions buried any remaining items.

6. Almost 1,400 years later, people knew of the buried city. No one paid much attention to it.

7. In 1748, a man was digging in a vineyard. His shovel hit a buried wall.

8. Italian historians were excited by the discovery. Archaeologists soon began to excavate, hoping to find important artifacts.

9. Archaeologists decided to leave many objects where they were found. They began restoring the site to its original condition.

10. After ongoing excavation, about three-fourths of Pompeii is visible. Visitors can see how the Pompeians lived.

Using Subordinate Clauses

DIRECTIONS Combine the pair of sentences into one.

- Make the second sentence a subordinate clause and attach it to the first sentence, following the clues given.
- You may need to cut a word or two from the second sentence.

EXAMPLE The banjo is an instrument. ~~This instrument~~ *that* became popular in the United States in the nineteenth century.

1. A banjo is a stringed musical instrument. It combines a guitar neck with a body like a tambourine. (Use *that*.)
2. The banjo was developed in Africa. It was brought to America. (Use *before*.)
3. The body of the banjo is covered with animal skin or plastic. The material is stretched over a round frame. (Use *that*.)
4. This body gives the banjo its characteristic sound. Its strings are plucked. (Use *when*.)
5. A five-string banjo's shortest string is fastened to a screw in the neck. This string is known as the "thumb string." (Use *which*.)
6. My sister decided to play the banjo. She listened to a famous banjo picker. (Use *after*.)
7. She has become an enthusiastic banjo student. She practices night and day. (Use *who*.)
8. Fingerpicking is a style of banjo playing. It is said to "sparkle." (Use *that*.)
9. My sister is good at frailing. Frailing is a way of strumming the banjo instead of picking it. (Use *which*.)
10. People cannot help but dance. Banjo players start strumming and picking. (Use *when*.)

Using Subordinate Clauses

DIRECTIONS Combine the pair of sentences into one.

- Make the second sentence a subordinate clause and attach it to the first sentence, following the clues given.
- You may need to cut a word or two from the second sentence.

EXAMPLE Newfoundland is an eastern Canadian province. ~~It~~ *that* is not heavily populated.

1. John Cabot, an Italian, discovered Newfoundland in 1497. Cabot explored for England. (Use *who*.)
2. He spread the word about the area. Fish were plentiful there. (Use *where*.)
3. Many fishing boats came from different countries. People heard the news. (Use *after*.)
4. Fishing crews competed for the area. They knew the area could supply a lot of food. (Use *which*.)
5. Communities of fishing camps existed for many years. The area finally became a colony in 1824. (Use *before*.)
6. Its people showed their strong independence. They refused to become Canadians until 1949. (Use *when*.)
7. Part of Newfoundland is an island. It is separated from the mainland by the Strait of Belle Isle. (Use *that*.)
8. The rest of Newfoundland is made up of the Labrador coast. This coast is part of the Canadian mainland. (Use *which*.)
9. Newfoundland's largest city is St. John's. St. John's is also the capital of the province. (Use *which*.)
10. The area has a wild, rugged seacoast. It stretches for 10,000 miles. (Use *that*.)

Revising a Paragraph by Combining Sentences

DIRECTIONS The following paragraph sounds choppy because it has too many short sentences. Use the methods you have learned in the "Combining Sentences" section to combine sentences in the paragraph.

- First, mark up the paragraph to show the revisions you will make.
- Then, rewrite the paragraph.

Atlantic puffins are seabirds. Atlantic puffins nest along northern seacoasts. They spend most of their adult lives far out at sea. They come to land only to nest. The parents dig a hole in the ground three to six feet deep. The female usually lays one white egg. Both adults incubate it for more than a month. The chick hatches. It stays warm under its parents' wings for a few days. Puffins can be identified by their bright beaks. They can be identified by their multi-colored beaks. "Sea parrot" is one nickname for these colorful birds. "Clown of the sea" is another nickname for them. "Bottlenose" is a third nickname. They are clumsy fliers. They are graceful and efficient swimmers. They propel themselves with their wings. They use their feet to steer. Puffins are comical in appearance. Puffins are talented fishers.

Revising a Paragraph by Combining Sentences

DIRECTIONS The following paragraph sounds choppy because it has too many short sentences. Use the methods you have learned in the "Combining Sentences" section to combine sentences in the paragraph.

- First, mark up the paragraph to show the revisions you will make.
- Then, rewrite the paragraph.

Gray meerkats are a type of mongoose. Gray meerkats live in the Kalahari Desert in southern Africa. Gray meerkats travel in groups. Gray meerkats hunt for insects during the day. Meerkats are small. Meerkats are often hunted by birds of prey. Meerkats have to dig for insects. They cannot watch for predators at the same time. For this reason, some meerkats hunt. Others stand guard. The guards take their job very seriously. The guards stay on constant lookout for danger. Later, other meerkats stand watch. The guards get a chance to eat. Cooperation is necessary for survival. Alone, meerkats are more vulnerable.

NAME ______ CLASS ______ DATE ______

Revising Stringy Sentences

DIRECTIONS Some of the following sentences are stringy and need to be improved.

- Revise them by (1) breaking each sentence into two or more sentences or (2) turning some of the complete thoughts into phrases or subordinate clauses.
- If the sentence is effective and does not need to be improved, write C for *correct*.

EXAMPLE ______ When Lightning streaks across the sky, ~~and~~ many people are fascinated.

______ **1.** Lightning is one of the most beautiful and spectacular events in nature.

______ **2.** Lightning can also be deadly, and lightning kills about 100 Americans every year.

______ **3.** Benjamin Franklin used a kite to help prove that lightning was made of electricity, but his experiment was very dangerous, and Franklin was lucky that he was not killed.

______ **4.** The safest place to be during an electrical storm is inside a building, or you can also take shelter inside a car, but be careful not to touch any of the metal parts.

______ **5.** Lightning can travel through telephone lines, and lightning can strike people through the phone, and because of this you should not use a telephone during a thunderstorm.

______ **6.** Lightning often strikes water, and it is dangerous to be in a pool during a thunderstorm, and that is why lifeguards clear the pool when they see lightning.

______ **7.** Since lightning usually strikes the tallest object in an area, it is dangerous to stand in an open field, on top of a hill, or on a beach during a thunderstorm.

______ **8.** Standing under a tall tree during a thunderstorm is not a good idea, and if lightning strikes the tree, it can jump from the tree to nearby objects.

NAME ________________ CLASS ________________ DATE ________________

Revising Stringy Sentences

DIRECTIONS Some of the following sentences are stringy and need to be improved.

- Revise them by (1) breaking each sentence into two or more sentences or (2) turning some of the complete thoughts into phrases or subordinate clauses.
- If the sentence is effective and does not need to be improved, write C for *correct*.

EXAMPLE ______ People like to change styles and one way they do this is by changing their hair.

______ **1.** Our hair does much more than keep our ears warm, and it can have a big effect on how we feel about ourselves, and it can be used to express our individuality.

______ **2.** We think our hair looks good, and we feel more confident, and we feel able to face the world.

______ **3.** All it takes is one bad haircut to make a person want to flee from society and hide under a bed until his or her hair grows out, and this can take a long time, since hair grows only about half an inch a month.

______ **4.** Hair can be changed with a snip of the scissors, and hair can also be changed by curling, straightening, or dyeing.

______ **5.** We can do so many different things with our hair, and because of this our hairstyles become a mode of self-expression, and people often make statements about who they are by how they style their hair.

______ **6.** Hardly any other part of our physical appearance can be changed as easily as our hair.

______ **7.** Some people like to do the opposite of what "everyone" is doing, and they wear unique hairstyles, and their hairstyles set them apart from the crowd.

______ **8.** Styles are as unique and individualized as the people wearing them, and different styles make the world more interesting.

NAME ______ CLASS ______ DATE ______

for **CHAPTER 18: EXERCISE 10** page 470 **PRACTICE A, WORKSHEET 23**

Revising Wordy Sentences

DIRECTIONS Some of the following sentences are wordy and need improvement.

- Decide which sentences are wordy and revise them. You can (1) replace a phrase with one word, (2) take out *who is* or *which is*, or (3) take out a whole group of unnecessary words.
- If a sentence is effective as it is, write C for *correct*.

EXAMPLE ______ Place a new toy in front of a baby and ~~see~~ watch what happens. ~~watching what the baby does with the new toy.~~

______ **1.** Being very curious, the baby will use all five of its senses to explore the new toy.

______ **2.** Our ancestors probably explored the world in much the same way, which is to say, using their senses to gain knowledge about their environment.

______ **3.** However, as far as learning about the moon was concerned, the moon was too far away for people to explore with any sense except sight.

______ **4.** Because of the fact that the moon changed, it was a natural subject for stories.

______ **5.** The Greeks and Romans thought that the moon was a goddess with three faces.

______ **6.** Early scientists offered a variety of explanations about life on the moon, and in fact, one scientist wrote that he believed the craters were built by moon creatures.

______ **7.** In 1609, Galileo, who was an Italian astronomer, became the first person to study the moon with a telescope.

______ **8.** Some people who were writers imagined traveling to the moon using antigravity devices or huge cannons to propel them.

______ **9.** The first moon landing, which took place in 1969, provided scientists with new information about the moon.

______ **10.** The astronauts brought back samples of rocks from the moon, proving completely and beyond a shadow of a doubt that the moon is NOT made of cheese.

Revising Wordy Sentences

DIRECTIONS Some of the following sentences are wordy and need improvement.

- Decide which sentences are wordy and revise them. You can (1) replace a phrase with one word, (2) take out *who is* or *which is*, or (3) take out a whole group of unnecessary words.
- If a sentence is effective as it is, write C for *correct*.

EXAMPLE ______ For some people, watching fish ~~swimming around~~ in ~~the water of~~ an aquarium is just not enough.

______ **1.** These people, who are eager to learn for themselves about aquatic life firsthand, would climb right into the aquarium if they could.

______ **2.** This desire to explore the world of fish and aquatic plants that live underwater gave birth to the sport of scuba diving.

______ **3.** Scuba diving, which is a relatively new sport, is becoming more and more popular.

______ **4.** Throughout the course of history, people have been diving in search of fish, shells, and treasure.

______ **5.** Up until the time at which scuba gear was invented, divers could stay underwater for only as long as they could hold their breath.

______ **6.** Some could stay under as long as three minutes, but this was dangerous because of the fact that divers can pass out underwater, endangering their lives.

______ **7.** Learning how to operate scuba gear requires lessons from a certified scuba instructor.

______ **8.** Public swimming pools and colleges sometimes offer courses of instruction that teach people to scuba dive.

______ **9.** In a scuba-diving course, you will learn that you should never go out on your own and scuba dive by yourself.

______ **10.** You will also learn how to avoid dangerous sea creatures that can harm you as a diver.

Adding Variety to Sentences

DIRECTIONS The following paragraph is uninteresting because it includes only compound sentences.

- Rewrite the paragraph to include a variety of sentence structures.
- In your version mix short, simple sentences; compound sentences; and longer sentences with subordinate clauses.

To become a fly fisher, you must master certain skills, and you must learn a lot about fish. You have to learn how to assemble your fly rod, and you must learn how to cast. You must cast the fly so that it drops onto the water like a snowflake, and you have to prevent the fishing line from slapping the water. It might not sound difficult, but novice fly fishers often spend hours untangling fishing line. You also need to learn where to find fish, and you must find out what these fish eat. It can all seem like a lot of work just to catch a fish, and the work can be hard. Catching that first beautiful trout makes all the work feel worthwhile, and you will think you have found the gold at the end of the rainbow!

NAME ______________________ CLASS ______________ DATE ______________

Adding Variety to Sentences

DIRECTIONS The following paragraph is uninteresting because it includes only compound sentences.

- Rewrite the paragraph to include a variety of sentence structures.
- In your version mix short simple sentences; compound sentences; and longer sentences with subordinate clauses.

Earth seems to be "solid as a rock," but its outer shell is actually made of rocky plates. The plates slide past each other slowly, and sometimes they collide. This motion creates great pressure on the outer edges of the plates, and this pressure builds up greatly. The rocks break under the strain and this creates an earthquake. The land that rings the Pacific Ocean is called the "Ring of Fire" and that is where most earthquakes occur. The largest earthquakes in the United States were in New Madrid, Missouri, and these occurred in the early 1800s. The largest of these New Madrid earthquakes was felt from Canada to the Gulf of Mexico, and this earthquake changed the course of the Mississippi River.

Revise a Paragraph by Improving Sentence Style

DIRECTIONS The following paragraph is hard to read because it contains stringy and wordy sentences.

- Revise the paragraph using the methods you have learned.
- Try to mix simple, compound, and complex sentences in your improved version.

Who can forget the thrill of the first time when you learned to ride a bicycle? However, the fact of the matter is that the thrill wears off as bicycles become our main transportation. As a result of what happens when we get older, once we get our driver's licenses, we don't even use our bicycles. Our bicycles are stored away in the garage, and they serve no purpose, and all they do is gather dust. Now, though, due to the fact that the mountain bike was developed, people are rediscovering the enjoyment and pleasure of biking that they first experienced as children. With its sturdy frame and knobby tires, the mountain bike is luring adults out to play, and it has brought bicyclists out in force to embrace and explore the land beyond the pavement. Mountain-bike trails wind through the nation's parks and wilderness areas and help adults satisfy the need to play and explore, which never really goes away and which stays with them forever.

Revise a Paragraph by Improving Sentence Style

DIRECTIONS The following paragraph is hard to read because it contains stringy and wordy sentences.

- Revise the paragraph using the methods you have learned.
- Try to mix simple, compound, and complex sentences in your improved version.

A dollar bill is just a piece of paper and has no value in and of itself and isn't worth anything. Dollar bills, as well as coins, checks, and credit cards, have value because we all agree that they have value. Before money was invented, people had to trade what they had for what they wanted, which was a system that was much less convenient than paying with money. This was known as the barter system, and people traded animal hides, cloth, animals, or other goods and services to get what they wanted, but the system did not always work. What if you went to the market to trade your goat for some chickens, and the person who had chickens to trade already had enough goats, and you would have to go home without a chicken? This problem is solved when there is an agreed-upon monetary system approved by society, providing a solution to the problems of the barter system. People accept money for the reason that they know that they can use the money to buy many different things. It's hard to imagine a world without some kind of monetary system. If money had never been invented, would people have to take along a couple of goats to the shopping mall when they went shopping instead of credit cards?

Identifying Main Ideas and Topic Sentences

DIRECTIONS Look for the main idea in each of the following paragraphs. Remember that the main idea is the overall point of the paragraph.

- If the selection has a topic sentence, underline it.
- If there is no topic sentence, write the main idea of the paragraph in your own words, using details from the paragraph.

1. Many people know an orca when they see one. Orcas have distinct black-and-white markings that make them easy to recognize. Commonly known as killer whales, they are a popular subject for documentaries and feature films. Frequently, orcas are featured performers in aquatic shows. Perhaps no other sea mammal is as familiar to people.

Main idea: ______

2. There are some common misconceptions about orcas. For one thing, they are not, as some people think, the largest species of whale. The orca is merely the largest member of the dolphin family of whales. Furthermore, many people think of orcas as solitary creatures, but they usually live in groups of up to fifty animals.

Main idea: ______

3. Killer whales hunt in organized groups. Working together, a group of killer whales can herd prey animals into shallow water, trapping them against the shore. Orcas' speed and body shape are ideal for hunting. Large, strong teeth and powerful jaw muscles help them seize large prey. Although they usually feed on fish and squid, they have been known to hunt successfully animals as large as great whales.

Main idea: ______

4. Orcas were once called whale killers, but the name has somehow been transposed to *killer whales.* Orcas are called killers not because of their behavior toward humans, but because of the way they treat other ocean creatures. They are fierce, quick, and intelligent predators with huge appetites. Orcas will hunt fish, squid, penguins, seals, whales, and other dolphins. Nonetheless, there are no records of an orca killing a human.

Main idea: ______

Writing a Topic Sentence

DIRECTIONS For each of the following paragraphs, write a topic sentence that communicates the main idea.

1. Before 1966, the ice axes used in mountain climbing had straight blades. This limited the kinds of slopes that could be climbed. When Yvon Chouinard added a slight curve to the pick side of the ax, however, even the steepest slopes seemed attainable. It was, indeed, the beginning of a new sport called *ice climbing*.

Topic sentence: ______________________________

2. The curved ice ax has allowed climbers to take on nearly vertical slopes that once seemed impossible. Now, armed with their axes, daring ice climbers prefer the extremely dangerous vertical slopes. Some of their favorite challenges are frozen waterfalls.

Topic sentence: ______________________________

3. Frozen waterfalls are intensely beautiful. Climbing on such ice is like climbing on a diamond that sparkles blue one minute and yellow the next. In addition, ice climbers get a breathtaking view of the winter world below them. Ice climbers also enjoy the challenges of frozen waterfalls. All the challenges of climbing an entire mountain can be encountered by scaling a single frozen waterfall.

Topic sentence: ______________________________

4. When ice climbers are on the side of a frozen waterfall, their arms and legs are in constant use. Each hand holds an ice ax. Strapped to each boot are crampons, which are a layer of two-inch spikes, some of which point forward to grip the ice. It takes strength to drive the ax into the ice. Even when a climber is not moving, each muscle is needed to hold on.

Topic sentence: ______________________________

5. Many experienced mountain and rock climbers shy away from this dramatic and dangerous sport. Those who do attempt the sport of ice climbing tend to be well prepared. They must have the right boots, gloves, spikes, and other equipment. While climbing, they are very slow and careful.

Topic sentence: ______________________________

Collecting Supporting Details

DIRECTIONS When you write paragraphs, you have to collect details that support your main idea. Practice with the following topic sentences. On the lines provided, list at least two details to support each topic sentence.

1. If I could organize a field trip, I know just where we would go.

Details: ______________________________

____

2. I have accomplished something important.

Details: ______________________________

____

3. Here is a person whom I consider successful.

Details: ______________________________

____

4. I'm the kind of person who says what I think.

Details: ______________________________

____

5. Cars have changed a lot since the 1970's.

Details: ______________________________

____

6. Last summer was different from all the summers before it.

Details: ______________________________

____

7. I hope to have an unusual career someday.

Details: ______________________________

____

8. I think everyone needs a pet.

Details: ______________________________

____

NAME ____________________ CLASS ____________ DATE ____________

for **CHAPTER 19: EXERCISE 4** ***page 481*** **WORKSHEET 32**

Developing a Clincher Sentence

DIRECTIONS For each of the following short paragraphs, write a sentence that can serve as its clincher, wrapping up the information presented in the paragraph, but not repeating it.

1. What animal is most closely associated with cold climates? It's probably the penguin. This is understandable because most penguins do live in very cold places, including the Antarctic. Some types of penguins, however, can tolerate warmer climates. One species even lives at the equator.

Clincher sentence: ____________________

2. There are several species of penguins, but a casual observer might not be able to tell them apart. One of the biggest differences is in their height and weight; they range from just over one foot tall and weighing two pounds to nearly four feet tall and weighing ninety pounds. Otherwise, they look basically the same. All are black and white, though some have tufts of yellow on their brow, and a few have streaks of yellow or orange on their upper body.

Clincher sentence: ____________________

3. Penguins cannot fly, of course, and from a distance they look as if they do not even have feathers. They do, however, have soft, downy feathers that keep them warm. They molt, or lose their feathers, once a year. While they are molting, they cannot go in the water. They stay in a sheltered area with other molting penguins.

Clincher sentence: ____________________

4. Their wings function as flippers; they use them to "fly" underwater. Penguins are efficient swimmers, and they are great fun to watch. When they are moving really fast, they leap out of the water to breathe, sometimes soaring three feet or more through the air.

Clincher sentence: ____________________

5. They are also fun to watch on land. They seem to waddle around but can move quite fast. On their home turf, they have to navigate their way around ice and rocks. Sometimes a penguin will flop on its belly and slide along, using its feet and wings to keep going.

Clincher sentence: ____________________

NAME CLASS DATE

for CHAPTER 19: EXERCISE 5 **page 482** **WORKSHEET 33**

Identifying Sentences That Destroy Unity

DIRECTIONS Each of the following paragraphs has one sentence that destroys the unity. Cross out the unrelated sentence.

1. The atmosphere on Venus is made up mostly of carbon dioxide and is heavier than the atmosphere on any other known planet. The average atmospheric pressure on Venus is ninety times greater than the average pressure on Earth's surface. Venus is the second planet from the Sun. If you stood on the surface of Venus, the amount of pressure on your body would be similar to the amount of pressure you would feel if you stood more than half a mile underwater on Earth.

2. Venus also experiences extreme temperatures. Venus is named for the goddess of love. The upper atmosphere goes from warm to extremely cold; it can vary from 25 degrees centigrade in the day to –150 degrees centigrade at night. The temperature increases, however, in the lower atmosphere. The planet's surface is unspeakably hot. It is hot enough to melt lead.

3. Venus's atmosphere is made up of thick clouds. Several layers of clouds surround the entire planet, and the layers move at different rates. The planet was called Phosphorus. The upper cloud layers move very rapidly, while the lower layers move more slowly. In fact, the upper clouds move about one hundred times faster than the lowest clouds.

4. Venus's cloudy atmosphere and extreme temperatures are related. The clouds that cover the planet reflect a lot of heat, so Venus absorbs less heat than Earth does. The heat that is absorbed is trapped and intensified by the clouds, and the surface temperature climbs. Radar images suggest that Venus may have sand dunes.

5. In the past, the dense cloud cover and turbulent atmosphere have made it difficult to see what the surface of Venus looks like. Venus rotates once every 243 Earth days. Scientists have been able to explore Venus, however. They have used spacecraft and radar to photograph and map the planet's surface.

NAME ______________________ CLASS ______________ DATE ______________

for **CHAPTER 19: EXERCISE 6** *page 485* **WORKSHEET 34**

Arranging Details by Using Chronological Order

DIRECTIONS Follow the directions for each item to practice telling about events in the order in which they happen.

1. **Tell a story.** Circle one of the following topics, and make up three or more events to include in a story about it. List the events in chronological order.

   - You have been assigned as supervisor to a group of eight-year-olds at an event.
   - It was an ordinary Monday until the principal announced that the school mascot was missing.
   - The room was an absolute wreck, and your parents were due to be home in two hours. You asked yourself, "How did I get into this mess?"

   Events:

   a. ______________________________

   b. ______________________________

   c. ______________________________

2. **Explain a process.** Circle one of the following activities. Then, list three or more steps involved in performing this activity. Arrange the steps in chronological order—that is, the order in which they should happen.

   - directing a visitor to the school cafeteria from your classroom
   - folding a paper airplane
   - teaching a dog a trick

   Steps:

   a. ______________________________

   b. ______________________________

   c. ______________________________

NAME ______ CLASS ______ DATE ______

for **CHAPTER 19: EXERCISE 7** *page 487* **WORKSHEET 35**

Arranging Details by Using Spatial Order

DIRECTIONS For each subject in the chart, list descriptive details and then arrange the details in spatial order.

LIST OF DETAILS	DETAILS IN SPATIAL ORDER
1. the most interesting landscapes you have ever seen	
2. your favorite place for doing homework	
3. the perfect clothes for hiking	
4. the oddest pet you have ever seen	
5. the most unusual motor vehicle you have ever come across	

NAME ______________________ CLASS ______________ DATE ______________

for **CHAPTER 19: EXERCISE 8** *page 488* **WORKSHEET 36**

Arranging Details by Using Logical Order

DIRECTIONS For each set of subjects in the chart, write down three ways that the two are alike and three ways that they are different.

TOPIC	ALIKE	DIFFERENT
1. vegetables and dessert	1. 2. 3.	1. 2. 3.
2. music your parents like and music you like	1. 2. 3.	1. 2. 3.
3. fun time with family and fun time with friends	1. 2. 3.	1. 2. 3.
4. team sports and individual sports	1. 2. 3.	1. 2. 3.
5. having a pet dog and having a pet goldfish	1. 2. 3.	1. 2. 3.

NAME ______________________ CLASS ______________ DATE ______________

for **CHAPTER 19: EXERCISE 9** page 489 **WORKSHEET 37**

Identifying Transitional Words and Phrases

DIRECTIONS Underline all of the transitional words and phrases in the following paragraphs.

1. "It's going to storm," warned Grandmother, pointing to birds way up in the afternoon sky. Only a few clouds were in sight, but I knew she was right. When a thunderstorm is forming, warm, moist air flows upward. Consequently, flying insects are drawn up, too. Because the insects are higher, birds must fly higher than usual to catch and eat them. As a result, the birds provide a sign that the atmosphere is right for developing thunderstorms. The swallows we saw were flying so high that we could barely see them. Grandmother and I therefore checked the TV weather forecast, and just as Grandmother thought, rain was expected.

2. Do you think crayons are just for little kids? Think again. Just about everyone, from preschoolers to professional artists, loves crayons. Crayons are so popular, in fact, that some clubs work to preserve their history. In 1991, for example, these clubs protested when several old crayon colors were replaced with new, updated colors. In addition to liking the colors themselves, people like the expressive names of some crayons, such as *purple pizzazz* for purple. People are also crazy about the scent of crayons. For example, their waxy smell is one of the top twenty scents recognized by adults. Clearly, crayons are not just for kids!

3. Add together a cloudless night, a group of campers, and several telescopes, and what do you have? A star party, of course. Star parties take place at national parks, state campgrounds, and observatories—anywhere far from light sources such as cities. The night sky has to be very dark for the stars to show up well. Before the party begins, a park ranger or astronomer explains which constellations or planets are visible at that time of year. When darkness finally arrives, the Milky Way splashes its 200 billion stars across the sky, and it's time for the party to begin. Campers step up to telescopes and focus. Suddenly, Saturn's rings seem huge and bright. The moon's craters look truly deep. When the stars begin to fade around dawn, campers stumble into tents to sleep all day.

Elaborating Details

DIRECTIONS The following paragraphs do not have enough elaboration. Rewrite each paragraph, adding details, facts, or examples to improve it.

1. Setting up a successful trip to the mall can be harder than it seems. First, you have to decide whether to go alone or with friends. Next, there is the matter of getting there. Most important, you have to have a good game plan about how to spend your time there.

2. It is really very easy to tell good movies from bad ones. Good movies have an interesting story and are fun to watch. Bad movies might have one or two good points, but when they are over, you find yourself saying, "Boy, that was stupid."

3. Families should prepare themselves for the possibility of extreme weather. Sometimes weather conditions result in a lack of electricity and water. It can even be hard to get fresh food. If people were prepared, then extreme weather would not seem like such a problem.

Identifying Types of Paragraphs

DIRECTIONS Answer the questions for each paragraph below.

1. This kitten has been in our house for only three weeks, but already it seems to belong to everyone. I always thought my brother Emil was my ally, but last night he proved me wrong. I heard meows and giggles coming from his room and went to investigate. I did not see them at first, but as I came around the bed I noticed the closet door was ajar. I opened it and there were the kitten and Emil, playing with my favorite ball!

Is this paragraph narrative, descriptive, expository, or persuasive? ______

How can you tell? ______

______

2. So tell me, why would anyone want a kitten? Cats have absolutely no intelligence. An animal with real intelligence knows how to fetch things like newspapers and balls. Cats require too much equipment, like litter boxes and scratching posts. Worst of all, they have no sense of loyalty. They rarely come when they are called. I say people should stick to nice, reliable pets such as dogs. I ought to know; I am one.

Is this paragraph narrative, descriptive, expository, or persuasive? ______

How can you tell? ______

______

3. Did you ever pay attention to cats' history? The earliest available records indicate that the Egyptians probably were the first to try to domesticate cats. Cats also appear in the art and literature of ancient cultures in Greece, Crete, China, and India. They were domesticated to keep rat populations down, and they have retained their hunting instinct. It is likely that they have always been self-reliant.

Is this paragraph narrative, descriptive, expository, or persuasive? ______

How can you tell? ______

______

NAME ______________________ CLASS ______________ DATE ______________

Dividing a Piece into Paragraphs

DIRECTIONS The passage that follows was originally broken into five paragraphs.

- Indicate where you think the paragraph breaks went—or should go—by underlining the first word of each paragraph.
- Then, explain your choices.

Have you ever been to a kite-flying contest? If you have, then you know that there are lots of unique and unusual kites being flown today. Kites come in all shapes and sizes and can be made with many different kinds of materials. Most people are familiar with the fairly simple diamond-shaped kites made of wooden sticks and paper. Kites, however, may be made of cloth or plastic and may be shaped like rectangles, triangles, squares, or even hexagons. Kites get their name from a bird called a kite. This hawklike bird glides on air currents while searching for prey. When it sees a mouse or an insect, it suddenly swerves, dips, or soars upward, chasing its prey. In a similar manner, a kite flown by people hovers in the sky and, with the jerk of a string, dives with a sudden whoosh or dances wildly across the sky. People in Asia have been flying kites as far back as recorded history. In some countries, such as China, Japan, Korea, and Malaysia, kite flying is a national pastime. Kites have symbolic significance in some of these countries and are flown on ceremonial occasions. An American famous for kite flying is Ben Franklin. According to legend, he hung a metal key on his kite line and flew the kite in a thunderstorm. As Franklin reportedly expected, the key attracted electricity from the air, providing evidence that lightning is electrical in nature. Because most people do not wish to be struck by lightning, modern kite flyers should think of Franklin's experience as a lesson about kite-flying conditions to avoid. Bad weather certainly can be dangerous to kite flyers, but it is not the only threat. Electrical wires can also be very hazardous. The best way to fly a kite is on a clear day, out in the open. The wind should be strong enough to keep the kite in the air, but not so strong that it will tear the kite to pieces. Ideally the wind should be between eight and twenty miles an hour. Never fly a kite in damp weather or near power lines.

Explanation for paragraph breaks:

____

____

____

____

Section 3: More Practice with Combining Sentences

NAME _______________ CLASS _______________ DATE _______________

Combining Sentence Parts

Sentences are made up of elements that come together to express an idea. The way you order these elements can affect how your reader understands the idea you are trying to express.

Notice how the following sentence parts are put together in an order that makes sense.

Sentence Parts: of both farmers and consumers
affecting the pocketbooks
hungry insects
damage crops

Combined: Hungry insects damage crops, affecting the pocketbooks of both farmers and consumers.

DIRECTIONS Combine the following sentence parts into one sentence. Insert punctuation and capitalize words as necessary.

1. many farmers
to increase their crop yields and their profits
use fertilizer

____

____

2. use chemicals
to protect their crops
to reduce the bollworm population
cotton farmers
but they also use insects

____

____

____

3. the cotesia wasp
the pirate bug
and even the fire ant
helpful insects include

____

____

4. one type of helpful insect
ladybugs are
that can control
aphids in the garden

____

____

5. in search of food
where they are placed
tend not to stay
ladybugs, however,
they fly away

6. is
it feeds on fast-moving insects
another helpful insect
the praying mantis

7. reduce the harmful insect population
but it also eats
the praying mantis can help
helpful insects

8. need to be studied
helpful insects
when and how they can best assist farmers
so we can better understand

9. is more effective
to protect crops
think that using natural means
some scientists
than using chemicals

10. more efficient and cost effective
whichever method
farmers will use
is

NAME CLASS DATE

LESSON 2

Using Semicolons

The **semicolon** (;) can connect the parts of a sentence to show that they are closely related. Use a semicolon only when two ideas are equally important and make better sense joined than separate.

Related Sentences: My neighborhood held a cleanup day for our park. We wanted to improve the park's appearance.

Combined: My neighborhood held a cleanup day for our park; we wanted to improve the park's appearance.

When the sentences are not closely related, you should leave them as two sentences.

Unrelated Sentences: Parks can be beautiful places. Squirrels can leap from tree to tree.

DIRECTIONS Read the following sentences and decide whether they should remain separate or be combined using a semicolon (;). Make capitalization changes as necessary. Make your changes on the worksheet.

- Use a semicolon to combine the sentences that should be combined.
- If the sentences do not need to be combined, write "no change" after the sentence.

EXAMPLE We went to the new baseball stadium; our favorite teams were playing.

1. Many people visit our park to relax and participate in sports. Children and adults alike are attracted to its many features.

2. During cleanup day, some people picked up trash along the creek. Others cleared the hiking trail.

3. Many cactus plants grow in the park. The park is located near the highway.

4. I helped a tree-planting crew. I carried water while other people dug holes.

5. Many trees had been damaged in a storm. We wanted to replace them to create shady areas.

6. Digging holes for the trees was strenuous work. We used both picks and shovels.

7. Our crew was fast and efficient. Each tree required five gallons of water.

8. We planted a small grove of oaks. They are already providing shade.

9. I already knew many of my neighbors. I had met them at neighborhood picnics.

10. Our hard work was worthwhile. My clothes got filthy from all the digging and kneeling on the ground.

11. Volunteer work has many rewards. It gives you a sense of accomplishment, and you get to watch people benefit from your hard work.

12. My sister volunteers at a soup kitchen. Helping people in need is her favorite part of the work.

13. My parents encourage us to help others in our community. We often go to my grandparents' house on weekends.

14. I think helping people through hard times is our duty. If people try to improve their situation, we should try to help them.

15. Next year I plan to volunteer at a kennel that trains dogs for the visually impaired. I'll be cleaning out dog pens and feeding the dogs.

16. Someday I hope to be able to help train dogs. Mom thinks dogs make better pets than cats.

17. Volunteer work at the kennel might even turn into a paying job one day. Getting paid to do work that helps others is my goal.

18. Regardless of the career I enter, I'll always do volunteer work. My sister wants to be a writer.

Using Colons, Dashes, and Parentheses

You may think of punctuation marks as tools to separate parts of sentences or paragraphs, but some punctuation marks can be used to join related ideas. These punctuation marks can therefore be used to combine sentences. Colons, dashes, and parentheses are three punctuation marks that can be used to combine sentences.

When one sentence lists a series of items that are introduced by an earlier sentence, consider combining the sentences with a colon.

Original: My brother has three favorite pastimes. They include eating, sleeping, and talking on the phone.

Combined: My brother has three favorite pastimes: eating, sleeping, and talking on the phone.

You can also use a colon to introduce a dramatic statement.

Original: I discovered exactly what I feared. Our boat anchor had come untied overnight.

Combined: I discovered exactly what I feared: Our boat anchor had come untied overnight.

You can use dashes and parentheses in several different ways to help vary your writing, changing your voice or a character's voice.

By using dashes, you can insert an idea right into the middle of another sentence.

Original: Rick watched TV the entire week at his cousins' house. Oh, how he missed his books!

Combined: Rick watched TV—oh, how he missed his books!—the entire week at his cousins' house.

A dash can also mean *namely, that is,* or *in other words.*

Original: As I finished running my first marathon, I could think of only one thing. I wanted to get off my feet.

Combined: As I finished running my first marathon, I could think of only one thing—getting off my feet.

Using parentheses allows you to include useful information that might be of only secondary importance.

Original: Some foods are not only easy to prepare but also nutritious. Vegetables are an example.

Combined: Some foods (vegetables, for example) are not only easy to prepare but also nutritious.

DIRECTIONS Combine each of the sets of sentences into a single sentence. You may need to add or delete words when combining the sentences.

- Combine the first three sets of sentences by using the punctuation mark that appears in italics at the end of the item.
- For the last three sentences, choose the punctuation mark (colon, dash, or parentheses) that you think is appropriate.

EXAMPLE The aurora borealis shimmered on the horizon. It is also called the northern lights. (*dash*)

The aurora borealis—also called the northern lights—shimmered on the horizon.

1. After three hours of baseball, we were all ready to go home. The game lasted twelve innings. (*parentheses*)

2. My friend from England says we should drive as the English do. They drive on the left side of the road. (*dash*)

3. The checklist for summer camp included several "essentials." The essentials included sunscreen, a hat with a wide brim, and mosquito repellent. (*colon*)

4. Our dog Banana won best of show at the kennel's weird-dog contest. He's pale yellow and has a perfectly curved tail.

5. The colors of the new band uniforms are a bit flashy for my taste. They are purple and silver.

6. Wandering aimlessly through the woods, I could almost hear the park ranger's advice. He said, "Don't forget your compass."

Using Connectors

Add variety to your sentences by using **connectors** to join sentences of equal importance. *And, but, or, for, yet,* and *so* are connectors.

Notice that when two sentences are combined, a comma comes before the connector.

Original: Traveling by train can be enjoyable. There are many faster ways to travel.

Combined: Traveling by train can be enjoyable, **but** there are many faster ways to travel.

DIRECTIONS Join the following sets of sentences by using the connectors *and, but, or, for, yet,* and *so*. The first five items are cued. For the last five, choose an appropriate connector. Make your changes on the worksheet.

EXAMPLE The heat was unbearable at the baseball game yesterday, and none of the drink machines were working. (*and*)

1. I took a nasty spill on my mountain bike. I wasn't seriously hurt. (*but*)
2. Heading down the rocky hill at a fast speed seemed okay. I had ridden the trail many times. (*for*)
3. I was surprised by the three-foot ditch that appeared in the middle of the trail. I still thought I could keep my bike under control by braking hard. (*yet*)
4. I realized I was still going too fast. I headed for the trees at the side of the trail. (*so*)
5. My handlebars must have clipped a branch. I might have gotten a twig in my spokes. (*or*)
6. Suddenly I was sailing through the brush headfirst. My bike, which was somewhere behind me, was making sounds you wouldn't expect from a bike.
7. I'm glad I was wearing a helmet. A tree brought my unexpected flight to a sudden stop.
8. Tree branches had scraped my arms and legs pretty badly. At least I didn't break any bones.
9. The front wheel of my bike was twisted like a pretzel. I had a long walk ahead of me.
10. I hoisted the bruised bike onto my shoulder. Riding the bike was no longer an option.

Using Paired Connectors

Add variety to your sentences by using paired connectors to join ideas of equal importance. When you use one connector, you usually use the other as well. Here are some common paired connectors:

either . . . or	not only . . . but also
neither . . . nor	both . . . and
whether . . . or	

The following combinations show the relationship between two sentences. You may need to change a word or two when you combine sentences. To indicate an additional important idea, use *not only . . . but also* or *both . . . and.*

Original: Volunteer work at the pool provided good work experience. Volunteer work at the pool gave me a good suntan.

Combined: Volunteer work at the pool **not only** provided good work experience **but also** gave me a good suntan.

To indicate a choice between alternatives, use *either . . . or, neither . . . nor,* or *whether . . . or.*

Original: The concert should have started earlier. The band shouldn't have played so long.

Combined: **Either** the concert should have started earlier**, or** the band shouldn't have played so long.

DIRECTIONS Use paired connectors to combine the following sets of sentences.

- For the first five items, use the paired connectors in italics at the end of each item.
- For the remaining items, use the paired connectors that best fit the meaning of the sentences.

EXAMPLE My favorite bookstore carries a wide variety of books. It has a great selection of magazines. (*both . . . and*)

My favorite bookstore carries both a wide variety of books and a great selection of magazines.

1. Last weekend I had to make a choice. I could go to the bookstore or the movies. (*whether . . . or*)

______

______

2. Some TV sitcoms are not well written. Some aren't funny. (*neither . . . nor*)

______

______

3. Jennifer is allergic to dogs. She is also allergic to cats. (*both . . . and*)

4. The horses are naturally high spirited. They're just frisky today. (*either . . . or*)

5. The storm provided some badly needed rain. It dropped temperatures. (*not only . . . but also*)

6. The local radio stations don't play classical music. They don't play jazz either.

7. The steamed vegetables smelled bad. The vegetables also tasted stale.

8. The city managers will hold another election. They will just drop the proposal.

9. Baseball requires a lot of strategy. Soccer requires a lot of strategy as well.

10. I had to choose. I could take Spanish or French.

NAME ________________ CLASS ________________ DATE ________________

LESSON 6

Using Adverb Connectors

Adverbs can be used to show special kinds of relationships between ideas. When you combine sentences with these adverbs, you make your meaning clearer and your style smoother.

- *However, instead, on the other hand,* and *nevertheless* show that one idea is followed by an opposite idea.
- *Therefore* and *consequently* suggest that a conclusion is being made.
- *Besides, furthermore,* and *moreover* signal that some additional point, idea, or detail will follow.
- *Indeed* and *in fact* help emphasize the writer's point.

These connectors need a semicolon before them, and a comma usually follows.

Original: I moved to North Carolina just before the hurricane hit. I saw the effects of two different hurricanes. (*in fact*)

Combined: I moved to North Carolina just before the hurricane hit**; in fact,** I saw the effects of two different hurricanes.

DIRECTIONS Join the following sets of sentences by using adverb connectors. Use the connectors provided for the first six items. For the remaining items, choose an appropriate adverb from the ones listed above. Make your changes on the worksheet.

EXAMPLE Some communities were devastated by these hurricanes; on the other hand, some escaped with little damage.

1. After hurricanes, Princeville, North Carolina, often receives enormous amounts of rainfall. One hurricane brought twenty inches of rain to the area. (*indeed*)

2. Many residents fled inland to avoid the flooding. Some stayed behind to protect their town. (*however*)

3. An earthen dam was built to protect the town. A flood covered Princeville. (*nevertheless*)

4. Princeville was under water for several weeks. Most of the town's homes were damaged. (*consequently*)

5. I lived in Raleigh. I was very worried about my friend Linda in Princeville. (*however*)

6. Linda grew up in Princeville. She could trace her family tree back to the town's founders. (*moreover*)

7. The town was founded after slavery ended. It was the first town in the United States to be governed by African Americans.

8. The people of Princeville were very proud of their town. Many wanted to stay and rebuild it.

9. Some people in Princeville said they would never again risk being in a flood. Others refused to leave their ancestral home.

10. Most of the town's citizens showed pride in their heritage. They expressed their determination to rebuild Princeville.

11. I had expected to see only discouragement in my friend's hometown. I saw a great deal of hope.

12. Linda's house was okay, but I decided to stay with her awhile. Disaster-relief agencies needed volunteers.

13. Linda and I joined a group that was helping clean mud out of people's houses. We bought tall rubber boots.

14. Washing mud out of houses with a water hose and sweeping with heavy brooms was hard work. Helping the community recover made us feel good.

15. Relief agencies came from around the country to help Princeville. One group came from Alaska.

16. I'm glad I was able to help my friend's community. I was very happy to return to a clean, dry Raleigh.

NAME ______ CLASS ______ DATE ______

Expanding and Combining with Modifiers

Modifiers are words that describe or limit other words. These are words that help you give precise information to your reader.

In these groups of sentences, modifiers have been moved into the first sentence from the sentence or sentences that follow. Sometimes a comma (,) or the word *and* needs to be added.

Original: New York City has a rich history. New York City has an interesting history.

Combined: New York City has a rich**, interesting** history.

Original: Travelers to New York City discover that the city is huge. They discover that it is always bustling with activity. These travelers are amazed.

Combined: **Amazed** travelers to New York City discover that the city is huge **and always bustling with activity**.

DIRECTIONS Study the examples and combine the following sentences. Mark your changes on the worksheet.

EXAMPLE New York City was the ^first capital of the United States. ~~It was the first capital~~.

1. The new city grew rapidly from the borough, or county, of Manhattan. The city was bustling.

2. New York City is made up of five boroughs. The five boroughs make up modern New York City. Each borough is unique.

3. Manhattan is the best-known borough, with its theater districts and universities. Its theater districts are famous. Its universities are respected.

4. Manhattan is also home to skyscrapers and artistic centers. The skyscrapers are enormous. Manhattan is home to musical centers. Manhattan's artistic and musical centers are world renowned.

5. Brooklyn has its own identity, with numerous waterfront and cultural areas. The waterfronts are bustling. There are various cultural areas.

6. Most housing in Manhattan consists of apartments. Most housing in Brooklyn consists of apartments.

7. In Queens, many residents live in homes and enjoy easy trips to sports stadiums and shopping centers. Most homes in Queens are family owned. Trips to sports stadiums and shopping centers are quick.

8. The northern area of the Bronx has become an important base for Puerto Rican immigrants, who have gained power by electing officials. They have increased their influence. They have elected Puerto Rican officials.

9. Despite Staten Island's population growth, it still contains mainly housing and natural areas. The population growth has been rapid. Staten Island's housing is private. Staten Island's natural areas are lovely.

10. These five boroughs have seen rapid changes in their political structures, and have provided a birthplace of ideas for the rest of the nation. These five boroughs are distinct. These five boroughs have seen rapid changes in their social structures. They have provided fresh ideas. They have provided challenging ideas.

Combining and Varying Sentences

If the songs of your favorite band all sounded the same, you would probably get tired of listening to them pretty quickly. No matter how well you like the band's songs, you expect to hear some variety when you buy one of their CDs. The same is true in writing: If your writing style never varies, your reader will soon become bored. Varying sentence structure is one way to keep your writing fresh and interesting.

The most common sentence structure begins with a subject followed by a verb.

Elena cooked dinner for her parents and their friends last Sunday afternoon.

The Internet has become one of the best research tools available.

The structure of these sentences—subject plus verb—is clear and precise, but if this pattern were repeated throughout a paragraph or more of text, the reader would soon grow tired of the same old rhythm. To keep your writing style energetic and engaging, vary your sentence structure by adding introductory words, phrases, and clauses to sentence beginnings.

Basic: The airplane veered frighteningly to the right after we took off.
Varied: Frighteningly, the airplane veered to the right after we took off.

Basic: The restaurant burned to the ground despite the fire department's quick response.
Varied: Despite the fire department's quick response, the restaurant burned to the ground.

Basic: My friend Jenny was excited about her late-summer trip to Scotland, even though it would cause her to miss the first week of school.
Varied: Even though it would cause her to miss the first week of school, my friend Jenny was excited about her late-summer trip to Scotland.

Basic: I hooked an old tire while fishing off the pier last week.
Varied: While fishing off the pier last week, I hooked an old tire.

DIRECTIONS Combine each set of the following sentences in two different ways, varying the beginnings of the sentences. You may need to add or delete words when combining the sentences.

EXAMPLE The band director raised his baton. Some of us didn't lift our instruments. He tapped loudly on his music stand to get our attention.

a. *When the band director raised his baton, some of us didn't lift our instruments, so he tapped loudly on his music stand to get our attention.*

b. *Because some of us didn't lift our instruments when he raised his baton, the band director tapped loudly on his music stand to get our attention.*

1. We ran three miles during gym class. It began to rain. Our track coach picked us up in the bus.

a. ____

____

b. ____

____

2. The lizard darted under a rock when it saw my cat creeping toward it. The lizard had already lost its tail in a previous encounter.

a. ____

____

b. ____

____

3. My remote-control airplane smashed into a utility pole before tumbling to the ground in a shower of plastic. Its flight ended suddenly.

a. ____

____

b. ____

____

4. The news broadcaster reported that the TV show had been canceled. He spoke in the same serious tone he might have used to report a tragedy.

a. ____

____

b. ____

____

5. The doctor strolled casually into the waiting room. He was unaware that he still had a cone-shaped birthday hat on his head.

a. ____

____

b. ____

____

LESSON 9

Using Prepositional Phrases

Reducing the number of words, phrases, and sentences in your drafts will help you focus on presenting clear, concise thoughts. You can use prepositional phrases to combine sentences and make your writing more concise, more interesting, and more powerful.

A **preposition** is a word that shows the relationship of a noun or a pronoun to some other word in a sentence. You can remember many prepositions by thinking about "anything that can be done to a mountain." For example, you can climb *over* a mountain, go *past* it, walk *to* it, be *near* it, be *in front of* it, be across *from* it, be *on* it, or go *down* it.

Some Common Prepositions

about	at	for	over
according to	below	from	past
across	between	in front of	to
after	by	near	under
along	down	off	up
around	during	on	with

A **prepositional phrase** includes a preposition, a noun or a pronoun, and any modifiers of that noun or pronoun.

Original: Shari used a pen to take notes. She took a pen *from her backpack.* She took notes *in English class.*

Combined: Shari took a pen **from her backpack** and used it to take notes **in English class.**

NOTE: Pay attention to the preposition *to.* When *to* is before a verb, it is the sign of an infinitive rather than a preposition. So, in the example above, *to take notes* is an infinitive phrase. If *to* follows a verb, as in the phrase *go to the mountain,* then it is a preposition.

DIRECTIONS For each of the following items, use prepositional phrases to create one sentence.

EXAMPLE Mark Twain wrote *Adventures of Huckleberry Finn.* The place where Twain wrote it is Connecticut.

Mark Twain wrote Adventures of Huckleberry Finn in Connecticut.

1. I chose to read *Adventures of Huckleberry Finn.* I read it for English class.

2. I like to read. I read between school and swim-team practice.

3. Much of the action in *Huckleberry Finn* occurs along the Mississippi River. The action occurs before the Civil War.

4. Huck Finn is a feisty kid whose life changes. His life changes during the story.

5. He gets an education and a new home. His home is in a well-meaning widow's house.

6. Huck's father kidnaps him. He takes him from the widow's house.

7. Huck escapes from his father. He hides on an island. The island is in the river.

8. He finds Jim, an escaped slave. He finds him on the island.

9. Huck and Jim find a raft. They find it floating by the island.

10. Huck helps free Jim. He helps free Jim from slavery.

NAME ______ CLASS ______ DATE ______

LESSON 10

Using Appositive Phrases

You may often find yourself writing a sentence only to explain something in a sentence you just wrote. You may combine the two sentences by turning the one that explains something into an appositive phrase.

An **appositive** is a noun or pronoun placed beside another noun or pronoun to rename or explain it. An **appositive phrase** is made up of an appositive and its modifiers.

Original: Gwen will miss the final basketball game because of an injury. Gwen is our best player.

Combined: Gwen, **our best player,** will miss the final basketball game because of an injury.

Notice that the appositive phrase *our best player* identifies or renames the noun *Gwen*. Using appositive phrases to combine sentences allows you to add information that makes your writing more polished and informative.

NOTE: Appositive phrases are set off by commas before and after the phrase.

Jordan, our paper's lead reporter, will spend career day at the city news office.

DIRECTIONS Combine the following sentences by making the second sentence into an appositive. Use commas where needed.

1. Rudyard Kipling lived from 1865 to 1936. He was a British poet and novelist.

______

______

2. Rudyard Kipling wrote many stories set in India. Kipling is the author of "Rikki-tikki-tavi."

______

______

3. "Rikki-tikki-tavi" was published in a book titled *Just So Stories.* "Rikki-tikki-tavi" is the story of a mongoose who saves a family by killing cobras.

______

______

4. A mongoose is fierce and lightning quick. A mongoose is an animal capable of killing poisonous snakes.

______

______

5. Mongooses live in southern Asia and in parts of Africa. Mongooses are wild but loyal animals.

6. *Just So Stories* was published in 1902. *Just So Stories* is a collection of children's animal fables.

7. Kipling drew the pictures for *Just So Stories*. He was an illustrator as well as a writer.

8. *The Jungle Book* is another book by Kipling. *The Jungle Book* is the story of a boy raised by wolves.

9. *Kim* is the story of an Irish orphan raised as an Indian. *Kim* is Kipling's best-known novel.

10. Kipling began his career as a newspaper editor. Kipling is the winner of the 1907 Nobel Prize in literature.

11. Kipling's son was killed in World War I. His son's name was John.

12. *Something of Myself* was published in 1937, after Kipling's death. *Something of Myself* is Kipling's unfinished autobiography.

NAME ______ CLASS ______ DATE ______

LESSON 11

Using Participial Phrases

One way to add excitement to your writing is to begin sentences with action.

The actor yelled "Geronimo!" as he crashed through the fourth-story window.

Crashing through the fourth-story window, the actor yelled "Geronimo!"

Although the two sentences give the same information, the second one is more exciting because it begins with action.

A **participial phrase** is a verb phrase, such as *crashing through the fourth-story window,* that functions as an adjective, in this case describing *actor*. A participial phrase consists of the participle itself (*crashing*) and any complements or modifiers it may have. To avoid choppy, boring writing, you can use participial phrases to combine sentences.

Original: My friend left the dinner table with tears in her eyes. She was mumbling something about onions.

Combined: **Mumbling something about onions,** my friend left the dinner table with tears in her eyes.

Original: Carlos swung wildly at the third pitch. He was blinded by the sun.

Combined: **Blinded by the sun,** Carlos swung wildly at the third pitch.

DIRECTIONS Combine the sets of sentences by creating participial phrases. The part to be inserted is underlined in the first five items.

- Set off participial phrases with commas.
- You may need to make minor wording changes when combining the sentences.

EXAMPLE We declined the offer of dessert. We <u>had already eaten two pies that day</u>.

Having already eaten two pies that day, we declined the offer of dessert.

1. The librarian <u>marched toward the periodicals with her fists clenched</u>. "Please don't cut pictures out of the magazines," she said sternly.

______

______

2. The grass around the apartment swimming pool served as a reminder of what can happen when a cooking grill is left unattended. It was <u>blackened by fire</u>.

______

______

3. My horse bucked wildly at the sound of the rattlesnake. He almost threw me and stepped on the snake at the same time.

4. The smoke jumpers showered and went to bed immediately after dinner. They were exhausted from three days of fighting forest fires and a twelve-mile hike back to their camp.

5. My sister rushed to complete her research paper for science class. She slapped at the computer keys as if it were their fault she was late.

6. The chorus lost concentration while waiting for the solos to end. They completely missed the conductor's cue.

7. My grandfather lectured me on the advantages of going to college. He used his most serious tone of voice.

8. I bought the third volume of Tolkien's *Lord of the Rings* trilogy before I had even finished the second volume. I was captivated by Frodo's adventure.

9. The president walked down the aisle of the crowded auditorium. He was waving cheerfully.

10. Our dog, Skye, sailed through the air after leaping from the diving board. He looked quite graceful until he hit the water.

NAME ______ CLASS ______ DATE ______

LESSON 12

Using Infinitive Phrases

Infinitives and infinitive phrases are incredible. An infinitive phrase is so versatile that it can be used as either a noun, an adjective, or an adverb. Using infinitive phrases allows you to quickly and easily combine ideas into good sentences.

An **infinitive** is the base form of a verb. Think of an infinitive as *to* + a verb. An infinitive can be used in three different ways: as a noun, an adjective, or an adverb.

Noun: She tried *to explain* the story.
Adjective: If you need help with the math homework, Miranda is the one *to ask.*
Adverb: The computer program will be difficult *to learn* without the manual.

An **infinitive phrase** consists of an infinitive and the words that modify or complement it (*to* + a verb phrase). The entire infinitive phrase may be used as a noun, an adjective, or an adverb.

Noun: The coach told us *to work out three times a week.*
Adjective: I need to find a pen *to write a note.*
Adverb: It is easy *to find my house.*

Infinitive phrases are useful because they are so versatile. You can use an infinitive phrase to add just about any sort of information you want your reader to know. Infinitive phrases can answer many questions, such as *who, what, where, when, how,* or *why.*

DIRECTIONS Use at least one infinitive phrase to combine each of the following sets of sentences into a single sentence. For the first five items, a sentence beginning is provided.

EXAMPLES There is something I like. It is browsing through the library.

I like to browse through the library.

Seth tells stories. He entertains his friends.

Seth tells stories to entertain his friends.

Advertisers may pay for celebrity spokespeople. They will win customers.

To win customers, advertisers may pay for celebrity spokespeople.

1. I have a new art project. I am creating advertisements.

My new art project is ______

______

2. I have a dream. I dream of working for an ad agency.

My dream is ______

3. All advertisements are designed with a purpose. Their goal is attracting the attention of the reader.

All advertisements are ______

4. An eye-catching ad format is important. It focuses a reader's thinking.

To focus ______

5. Many ads are designed with a purpose. They make readers laugh.

Many ads are designed ______

6. Often a funny message will help readers. Readers remember the product.

______

7. I have a plan. I will build an art studio in my backyard.

______

8. First, I will need my mother's permission. I'll dig up part of her garden.

______

9. We'll need a compromise. I will accomplish my goal.

______

10. Once the studio is built, I'll have plenty of space. I will create my art.

______

Using Gerund Phrases

Is running your favorite sport? Do you enjoy eating? Is swimming on the top of your list? Do you notice how these *-ing* words don't seem to be acting like verbs all the time? Well, that is because they are gerunds.

A **gerund** is a verb form ending in *-ing* that is used as a noun—a person, place, thing, or idea. In the following sentence, notice that Jake will be doing *something* on Thursday night. The *something* is an *-ing* verb used as a noun.

Jake will be *babysitting* on Thursday night.

A **gerund phrase** consists of a gerund and any modifiers and complements it may have. The entire gerund phrase can do anything a noun can do.

Reading about science is Marlo's favorite pastime.

Gerunds can add action to your sentences. Two choppy sentences combined with a gerund phrase become one direct statement. Notice that when you combine sentences using a gerund phrase, you may need to delete some words and change or move others.

Original: I learned the swan dive. It was fun.
Combined: **Learning the swan dive** was fun.

A gerund phrase may be placed anywhere that a noun could be in a sentence.

Original: Alexa swims every day. It is her favorite activity.
Combined: **Swimming every day** is Alexa's favorite activity.
Combined: Alexa's favorite activity is **swimming every day.**

DIRECTIONS Combine each of the following sets of sentences into one sentence, using gerund phrases. The underlined verb should begin the gerund phrase.

EXAMPLE Abe practiced his speech. It helped him feel confident.

Practicing his speech helped Abe feel confident.

1. We hiked all day. It was exhausting.

____

2. I chose my research project. It took a great amount of time.

____

3. We rode our bikes fifteen miles. It exhausted both of us.

____

4. My mother has a business. She bakes bread.

5. I run the 20-yard dash on the track team. It is fun.

6. We looked at cells under a microscope during biology class. I enjoyed it.

7. I auditioned for a play. It proved to be easier than I had thought.

8. We practiced the medley many times in choir. It was necessary.

9. I learned a new dance. It challenged my partner and me.

10. My brother volunteers. He reads aloud for visually impaired people.

11. I play the kazoo. It is my hobby.

12. We camped at the Grand Canyon. It was exciting.

13. I mow yards. It helps me earn money for school.

14. I read *Where the Red Fern Grows*. It made me sad.

15. We learned a Hungarian folk dance. It was interesting.

Using Subordinating Conjunctions

Connecting words called **subordinating conjunctions** allow you to join ideas that are not of equal importance. Words such as *as, because, although, since, after, before, if, until, when,* and *as soon as* make the less important idea in a sentence depend on the more important one.

Combining pairs of sentences with a subordinating conjunction will help your ideas flow more smoothly.

Notice that if you place your subordinating conjunction at the beginning of the sentence, you should use a comma after the **clause,** a group of words that contains a subject and a verb and is used as part of a sentence. Sometimes, you may need to drop or change words to make your new sentences read correctly.

Original: Scientists cannot fully understand why we need sleep. They must do a great deal of research. *(before)*

Combined: **Before scientists can fully understand why we need sleep,** they must do a great deal of research.

Original: Most people do not think about the process of sleep. They think about sleep only when they do not get enough of it. (*until*)

Combined: Most people do not think about the process of sleep **until they do not get enough of it.**

DIRECTIONS Use a subordinating conjunction to combine the following sets of sentences. For the first five items, use the conjunction that is provided. Choose an appropriate conjunction for the last five items.

1. My soccer coach always reminds me to get plenty of sleep the night before a morning game. I'm usually too nervous to sleep. (*although*)

____

____

2. My lack of sleep becomes apparent about halfway through the game. I begin to lose my concentration and make bad passes. (*when*)

____

____

3. I expect to make varsity squad in a couple of years. I'll need to change my training habits, including my sleeping habits. (*if*)

____

____

4. Sleep probably won't be as much of a problem on the varsity squad. Their games are usually in the afternoon or evening. (*because*)

5. I made several bad passes during Saturday's game. My coach probably didn't think I was varsity material. (*after*)

6. The game was over. I got on the team van and immediately fell asleep.

7. The honking horn on the van woke me up. I was dreaming about playing in a World Cup match.

8. I quickly came back to reality. My coach was glaring at me disapprovingly.

9. His glare melted into a sly grin. I said, "Hey, coach, I did score the winning goal, remember?"

10. I scrambled out of the van and headed for my house. I wondered whether David Beckham ever slept through a game.

Using Adverb Clauses

When you are writing, there can be many questions to answer for readers. You may write a sentence to answer each question. However, you may choose to answer some of them within one sentence by using adverb clauses. (Remember that a **clause** is a group of words that contains a subject and a verb and is used as part of a sentence.)

An **adverb** modifies a verb, an adjective, or an adverb.

Bravely, Amelia climbed the high-dive ladder. (The word *bravely* explains how Amelia climbed.)

An **adverb clause** is a subordinate clause that modifies a verb, an adjective, or an adverb.

Because Amelia was brave, she climbed the high-dive ladder. (Now an entire clause explains how Amelia climbed.)

Adverb clauses help you combine ideas into one sentence by answering the following questions: *How? When? Where? Why? To what extent? How much? How long?* and *Under what condition?* When you combine sentences with adverb clauses, you use words called **subordinating conjunctions.**

Some Common Subordinating Conjunctions

after	although	as	as if	as soon as
because	before	if	since	so that
though	unless	until	when	whenever
where	wherever	while		

Original: I can't concentrate in a noisy room. I can't concentrate on my homework.

Combined: **If the room is noisy,** I can't concentrate on my homework. *(tells under what condition you can't concentrate)*

Original: I haven't finished my homework. I can't go to the game.

Combined: **Since I haven't finished my homework,** I can't go to the game. *(tells why you can't go)*

NOTE: When an adverb clause is at the beginning of a sentence, place a comma after it.

DIRECTIONS Combine the following sentences by turning one sentence into an adverb clause using the subordinating conjunction provided. You may need to delete or rearrange words.

1. It is hot. I like to swim. (*when*)

2. I smell popcorn. I want to go to the movies. (*whenever*)

____

3. I'll finish my chores. I'll go to the park with you. (*as soon as*)

____

4. I am rearranging my room. I'll have a place to study. (*so that*)

____

5. I will stay at home. You will call. (*until*)

____

6. I'd like to go to the basketball game. I already have plans. (*although*)

____

7. I talked to Mia. I called you. (*before*)

____

8. I will eat almost anything. I can't eat food that is spicy. (*unless*)

____

9. We go a lot of places. Brady knows people everywhere. (*wherever*)

____

10. I don't eat. I watch TV. (*while*)

____

11. Gwen looks tired. She looks like she has run a marathon. (*as if*)

____

12. We saw you. We went to the art gallery. (*after*)

____

13. I read the book. I'd like to see the movie. (*since*)

____

14. Basketball practice will get out early. We'll go to the play. (*if*)

____

15. I will finish my homework. I will call you. (*after*)

____

Using Adjective Clauses

Combining sentences using **clauses**—a group of words that contains a subject and a verb and is used as a part of a sentence—will save you time and trouble. Without an adjective clause, you may have to write a whole sentence just to explain another sentence.

Original: Marguerite likes to travel to visit relatives. Marguerite was born in Mexico.

Combined: Marguerite**, who was born in Mexico,** likes to travel to visit relatives.

An **adjective clause** is a subordinate clause that modifies a noun or a pronoun. Adjective clauses usually begin with one of the following words.

that *where* *when* *which* *who* *whom* *whose*

These introductory words should be positioned near the word or words that the adjective clause modifies. In the example above, the adjective clause provides more information about Marguerite, so *who* is placed after *Marguerite.*

NOTE: Clauses that can be taken out of a sentence without changing the meaning are called **nonessential.** Nonessential clauses are set off with commas. Clauses that are **essential** to a sentence's meaning are not set off by commas. When combining sentences using adjective clauses, ask yourself if the sentence makes sense without the clause. If the answer is *yes,* then set off the clause with commas.

Essential: The class **that I like most** is Art.

Nonessential: Art**, which is the class I like most,** is the last period of the day.

DIRECTIONS Combine the following sets of sentences by using adjective clauses. Add commas when necessary.

1. *The Call of the Wild* is an adventure novel. The novel examines how environment shapes a character. (*that*)

____

____

2. The main character is a dog. The dog is stolen from his California home. (*that*)

____

____

3. The dog lives a comfortable life with Judge Miller. The dog's name is Buck. (*whose*)

____

____

4. A thief sends Buck to Alaska. The thief needs to pay his debts. (*who*)

5. Buck leads a sled team. Buck is big and strong. (*who*)

6. Buck is rescued by John Thornton. John Thornton treats the dog kindly. (*who*)

7. The dog and the man develop a strong bond. The bond often occurs between humans and animals. (*which*)

8. Buck hears a call. He cannot resist the call. (*that*)

9. Buck begins to follow a wolf. He sees the wolf in the forest. (*that*)

10. Eventually, Buck joins the wolves in the wild. Buck loses his friend Thornton. (*who*)

11. Jack London spent time living and working in Alaska. Jack London wrote *The Call of the Wild*. (*who*)

12. *White Fang* also follows a dog's life in Alaska. *White Fang* is another Jack London novel. (*which*)

Using Noun Clauses

English allows a word or a group of words to be used in many ways. For example, a **clause**, a group of words that contains a subject and a verb and is used as a part of a sentence, may function as a single part of speech. Your full name has more than one word: a first, a last, and perhaps even a middle name. However, even if you have three or four names, they all count as you, a single noun.

Remember that a **noun** is a word used to name a person, place, thing, or idea. A **noun clause** is a group of words used as a noun. Noun clauses can appear anywhere that a noun can.

Subject:	*What I said* caused people to applaud.
Direct Object:	My father asked me *what I said.*
Indirect Object:	The student election will give *what I said* a chance to be heard.
Object of a Preposition:	I can raise awareness with *what I said.*

When you use a noun clause to combine sentences, you will usually need to introduce the clause with one of the following words:

who	*which*	*when*	*why*	*that*
whom	*what*	*where*	*how*	

Original: Kyle told me something. Our team is meeting in the city gym.

Combined: Kyle told me **that our team is meeting in the city gym.**
Kyle told me **when our team is meeting in the city gym.**
Kyle told me **whom our team is meeting in the city gym.**

Noun clauses are useful for combining sentences because you can provide more specific information in one sentence. Noun clauses also help you to add variety to your sentence structures.

DIRECTIONS For each of the following items, finish the sentences by creating a noun clause.

- For the first nine items, use the italicized words to create noun clauses.
- For the last three items, choose one of the introductory words above to create noun clauses.
- Insert each noun clause into the appropriate blank.

1. Our class was given an assignment to research ______________________.

- national monuments are built. (*how*)

2. Our teacher told us ______________________ and ______________________.

- We should look for information. (*where*)
- We could ask for help. (*whom*)

3. My group wanted to know ____________________ and ____________________.

- The Statue of Liberty was built. (*how*)
- It was given to the United States. (*why*)

4. We also did not know ____________________.

- Someone designed the Statue of Liberty. (*who*)

5. Our group decided ____________________.

- Someone would go to the library. (*who*)

6. I asked the librarian ____________________.

- I should look for information. (*where*)

7. I found a guidebook and read ____________________ and ____________________.

- Alexandre-Gustave Eiffel designed the statue's framework. (*that*)
- Frederic Bartholdi designed the rest of the statue. (*that*)

8. We learned ____________________.

- The Statue of Liberty is actually named *Liberty Enlightening the World*. (*that*)

9. ____________________ had never occurred to me.

- The Statue of Liberty is important. (*why*)

10. A poem on the statue explains ____________________.

- Immigrants are welcome in the United States.

11. We discovered ____________________. Her name is Emma Lazarus.

- Someone composed the poem on the statue.

12. In our report we told our classmates ____________________ and ____________________.

- The creators of the statue valued democracy.
- It is a symbol of freedom.

Combining Sentences to Write a Paragraph I

Combining sentences in a variety of ways will allow you to communicate using natural, flowing language. This will help your readers more fully understand your ideas.

DIRECTIONS Read the following sentences; then, write a paragraph using the sentence-combining techniques you have learned. Begin your paragraph by describing beluga whales in the St. Lawrence River. Then, explain and offer a conclusion about the topic. You may change or delete words as needed, but your changes should not alter or delete any facts from the provided information.

1. Beluga whales live in Canada's St. Lawrence River.
2. Belugas can grow to be fifteen feet long and weigh three thousand pounds.
3. Belugas are white.
4. About ten thousand whales lived in the river in the early 1900s.
5. The whale population has steeply declined.
6. Researchers are not sure how many whales now live in the river.
7. The whales were once hunted for oil.
8. This caused the overall population of whales to drop.
9. The whales have been exposed to pollution.
10. Pollution may be the cause of the whales' high cancer rate.
11. These whales are classified as endangered.
12. Some scientists want belugas to receive even more protection.

NAME CLASS DATE

Choosing How to Combine

In these exercises, you are learning specific methods of combining sentences. Sometimes, in your own writing, you may want to use several methods at once to combine sentences. When you combine choppy sentences into one sentence, the images and ideas in your writing become more vivid and clear.

When you have a series of ideas that you want to combine into one sentence, begin by deleting repeated words and phrases. Then, combine the remaining ideas. Remember that pronouns can take the place of deleted words and phrases.

Original: My dog is small and energetic. My dog enjoys running. My dog greets us when we come home.

Combined: My dog, **who** is small and energetic, enjoys running **to greet** us when we come home.
(combined by inserting an adjective clause and an infinitive)

Original: My dog is easily frightened by loud noises. Loud noises come from the road near our house.

Combined: **However,** he is easily frightened by loud noises **that** come from the road near our house.
(combined by inserting a conjunctive adverb and an adjective clause)

DIRECTIONS Combine the following sets of sentences. Use any of the combining methods you have learned.

1. A truck was driving past our house. The truck was large. It bounced over the road.

2. My dog trembled at the noise. He trembled terribly. The noise was loud.

3. I made an appointment with my veterinarian. I asked whether we could help my dog. I asked if we could help my dog overcome its fear of loud noises.

4. She suggested an obedience school. The obedience school is local. Several of her patients attend the school.

5. I signed up for a six-week course at the obedience school. I used my allowance money. The course is for owners and pets.

6. I liked the people at the school. The people were friendly. The people took time to get to know my dog.

7. Pets had to participate in the training sessions. Owners had to participate in the training sessions.

8. The trainers helped my dog. The trainers suggested techniques. I could use the techniques at home.

9. We have had several lessons. My dog is less afraid of noises. My dog is brave.

10. My dog also learned how to do some tricks. The tricks are amusing. The tricks are speak, roll over, and dance.

11. We had a good experience with the school. I would recommend it to my friends. I would recommend it to friends who have dogs.

12. I would like to take more classes at the school. I want to learn about dog training. I want to learn about dog training as a career.

NAME ______________________ CLASS ______________ DATE ______________

LESSON 20

Combining Sentences to Write a Paragraph II

DIRECTIONS Read the following sentences. Then, write a paragraph by combining the sentences. The sentences follow the order of the paragraph. Combine the ideas to write a smooth and clear paragraph. The paragraph should explain how to read a poem to an audience.

1. These guidelines will help you.
2. They will help you read poetry aloud.
3. First, read the poem several times.
4. Think about what each word means.
5. Think about what the poem means to you.
6. Reading a poem aloud may help you understand it.
7. This is because a poem has rhythm.
8. You are reading the poem aloud.
9. The punctuation tells you when to stop.
10. The punctuation adds to the rhythm.
11. There is no punctuation at the end of a line. Don't stop.
12. You see dashes.
13. Expect a sudden shift in idea or thought.
14. This is the most important thing.
15. Try to express the meaning of the poem.
16. Try to express the meaning to your audience.

HOLT

Elements of

Language

FIRST COURSE

Think as a Writer: Interactive Writing WorkText

Writing Practice for Chapters 20–26

- Journal Warm-ups
- Writing Prompts
- Critical Thinking Mini-Lessons
- Revising and Proofreading

HOLT, RINEHART AND WINSTON
A Harcourt Education Company
Orlando • Austin • New York • San Diego • London

Table of Contents

Table of Contents *(continued)*

Table of Contents *(continued)*

Table of Contents *(continued)*

Chapter 25: Convincing Others

PREVIEW WRITING WORKSHOP
(Student Edition pp. 686–717)

Chapter 26: Advertising

PREVIEW WRITING WORKSHOP
(Student Edition pp. 718–751)

About This Book

Introduction: Thinking About Writing

The Blackline Masters

Both **Your Writing Process** and **Strategies for Evaluating and Revising** on pages 1 and 2 are helpful guides that can be used to improve writing not only in language arts but in all subjects. Keep copies of these pages in your subject notebook and refer to them whenever you read or begin a writing assignment.

When you come across a Proofreading worksheet, use the **Guidelines for Proofreading** on page 3 to help you determine what corrections to make.

Use the **Symbols for Revising and Proofreading** on page 4 when you correct the following worksheets in this booklet:

- **Focus on Word Choice**
- **Focus on Sentences**
- **Proofreading**

The Chapter Previews

Journal Warm-ups

At the beginning of each chapter is a Journal Warm-up. These warm-ups give you an opportunity to make a personal connection to the chapter. Small stories and journal-writing assignments help you to get started writing as you begin the chapter activities.

The Writing Workshops

The Worksheets

For each activity in the writing process, from Prewriting to Proofreading, you are given a chart or graphic organizer to help you plan, organize, and revise your work.

- **Prewriting** worksheets will help you work through steps before beginning to write your drafts. A writing framework will guide you through writing your final draft.
- Additional **Writing Prompts** include writing ideas about careers and other school subjects.
- A **Revising** form gives you a way to review your draft and find problems and solutions.
- **Revising Practice** gives you an early, incomplete draft, which you can use to practice both elaborating and organizing.

A practice worksheet is provided for each **Mini-Lesson** and each **Focus on Word Choice** or **Focus on Sentences**.

Your Writing Process

Before You Write

Prewriting

- Choose a **form** for your writing and a manageable **topic.**
- Identify your **purpose and audience.**
- Draft a sentence that expresses your **main idea.**
- **Gather information** about the topic.
- Begin to **organize** the information.

While You Write

Writing

- Draft an **introduction** that gets your reader's attention and states your main idea.
- Provide **background information.**
- State your **supporting points** and **elaborate** on them.
- Follow a **plan** or order.
- Wrap things up with a **conclusion.**

After You Write

Revising

- **Evaluate** your draft.
- **Edit** the draft to improve its content and style.

After You Have Written

Publishing

- **Proofread** the draft to find and correct spelling, punctuation, and grammar mistakes.
- **Share** your finished writing with readers.
- **Reflect** on your writing experience.

Strategies for Evaluating and Revising

Evaluate Your Draft

- **Re-read.** Re-read your draft carefully—not once, but several times—focusing on content, organization, and style.
- **Ask.** Ask a peer to read the draft, point out weak or confusing parts, and make suggestions.

Content and Organization

- **Add.** Add sensory or factual details, examples, and illustrations.
  Add words and phrases (such as *as a result, for example, first,* and *however*) to connect ideas.
- **Delete.** Delete words, sentences, and paragraphs that stray from your thesis.
  Delete padding—unnecessary words and repetition.
- **Replace.** Replace elements that don't work as well as they should.
  Replace a weak piece of support with one that backs up your main idea more effectively.
- **Rearrange.** Rearrange sentences and paragraphs to find the clearest order of ideas.
- **Elaborate.** Elaborate and support each main point by providing specific details, facts, examples, illustrations, sensory images, figurative details, quotations, or anecdotes.

Revise for Style

- **Eliminate.** Eliminate slang, clichés, and worn-out verbs.
- **Avoid.** Avoid using the passive voice.
- **Vary.** Vary sentence length and sentence beginnings.
- **Combine.** Combine sentences to add variety or complexity.

Guidelines for Proofreading

	Yes	No	Needs Work
1. Is every sentence a complete sentence, not a fragment or run-on?			
2. Does every sentence begin with a capital letter? Does every sentence end with the correct punctuation mark? Are punctuation marks used correctly within sentences?			
3. Do all plural subjects have plural verbs? Do singular subjects have singular verbs?			
4. Are verb forms and tenses used correctly?			
5. Are adjective and adverb forms used correctly in comparisons?			
6. Are the forms of personal pronouns used correctly?			
7. Does every pronoun agree with its antecedent (the word it refers to) in number and gender? Are pronoun references clear?			
8. Are all words spelled correctly?			

Symbols for Revising and Proofreading

Symbol	Example	Meaning of Symbol
≡	Tucker's homestyle Restaurant (≡ under h)	Capitalize a lowercase letter.
/	the ~~C~~ity of Raleigh	Lowercase a capital letter.
‸	a cup‸milk (of inserted)	Insert a missing word, letter, or punctuation mark.
℘	How's the ~~that~~ apple?	Leave out a word, letter, or punctuation mark.
∽	frist	Change the order of letters or words.
¶	¶ "Go ahead," he said.	Begin a new paragraph.
⊙	She wept⊙	Add a period.
‸,	I still apologized‸, however.	Add a comma.

NAME ______ CLASS ______ DATE ______

Journal Warm-up: Eyewitness Account

When the thick smoke cleared, the battlefield was covered with twisted bodies. This year's Civil War reenactment took place on the hottest day of summer. Actors in woolen Civil War uniforms gladly shuffled off the field for a cool drink of water.

The first time I marched in a parade we all nearly drowned in the rain. Soaked crepe paper that felt like soggy corn flakes covered the ground. My clarinet croaked and squeaked with dampness. Spectators cheered us from beneath bright umbrellas and raincoats.

JOURNAL STARTERS

Write an eyewitness account for five minutes, using one of these prompts.

- Describe a party or picnic you attended.
- Tell about meeting or seeing a famous person.
- Describe an exciting play in a game you saw.
- Give an account of a recent visit to a museum.
- Describe the sounds, sights, and smells of a typical Saturday in your neighborhood.

NAME ____________ CLASS ____________ DATE ____________

for **CHAPTER 20: YOUR TURN 4** ***page 514***

Prewriting: Choosing an Experience

DIRECTIONS Use the graphic organizer to choose an experience for your eyewitness account.

STEP 1: Brainstorm a list of events you have witnessed. Consider sports events, school events, natural events, neighborhood events.

STEP 2: Which events . . .

- were most interesting?
- do you remember most clearly?
- did you see from beginning to end?
- did you observe without participating in?

STEP 3: Choose the event you most want to write about.

The event is ____________.

Prewriting: Identifying Your Audience

DIRECTIONS Use the graphic organizer to determine the audience for your eyewitness account.

I chose to describe an eyewitness account of

Who did not witness the event but might like to read about it?

1.

2.

3.

Who else would be interested in the event?

1.

2.

3.

I will write my eyewitness account to ______.

NAME CLASS DATE

for CHAPTER 20: YOUR TURN 6 **page 516**

Prewriting: Gathering and Organizing Ideas

DIRECTIONS Use the chart below to gather and organize ideas for your eyewitness account.

- In the first column, write the events of your experience in chronological order.
- In the second column, identify details for each event.
- Use additional paper if necessary.

Eyewitness Account: ____________________

EVENTS	DETAILS: Who? What? Where? How?
Event 1:	
Event 2:	
Event 3:	
Event 4:	

NAME ______________________ CLASS ______________ DATE ______________

Showing Instead of Telling

DIRECTIONS Rewrite the following *telling* statements as descriptive *showing* statements. Use dialogue, precise words, and figures of speech such as similes and metaphors.

1. It was a lovely day.

2. My sister is a good cook.

3. She enjoyed the dancing.

4. My cousin Ryan is shy.

5. Folk music is my favorite music.

6. Mona was really sad when her best friend moved away.

7. Swimming is a good way to relax.

8. The new video game is awesome.

NAME _______________ CLASS _______________ DATE _______________

for **EYEWITNESS ACCOUNT** *page 518*

Writing: Writing Prompts

DIRECTIONS Choose your own event for your eyewitness account, or use one of the following prompts.

WORKPLACE

Your friend belongs to a rock climbing club. She will be away for a month and has asked you to sit in for her at a meeting and jot down notes about everything that happens, including members' concerns and any new ideas discussed. Write her a letter giving an eyewitness account of the meeting.

SCHOOL

Your school maintains a Web site that allows online visitors to learn more about the school. The goal of the Web site is to promote a positive image of your school, its students, and their activities. Write a letter to parents who may be looking at the site. Give an eyewitness account of a school event.

MUSIC

The school choir and band spend weeks rehearsing a piece before performing it. The musicians practice the music over and over until it is nearly perfect. Visit a rehearsal of the school choir or band, and later watch its final performance. Then, write a letter to a friend including an eyewitness account of what you saw and heard.

PHYSICAL EDUCATION

Every year at your school, you and your classmates are challenged to pass the Presidential Physical Fitness exam. Your classmates have all been training for a month by practicing sit-ups, sprints, pull-ups, and long jumps. Write a letter to the local or school newspaper giving an eyewitness account of your classmates' preparation for the Presidential Physical Fitness test.

SOCIAL STUDIES

Your social studies class is focusing on democracy and the election process. Your teacher has made the process more interesting by having your class hold a mock convention with candidates preparing campaigns, giving speeches, and debating issues. Write an eyewitness account of the mock convention in a letter to a relative who is interested in politics and government.

NAME ______________________ CLASS ______________ DATE ______________

Writing: Drafting Your Eyewitness Account

DIRECTIONS Complete the graphic organizer below, and use it to help you write your first draft. Use additional paper if necessary.

INTRODUCTION

What salutation will you use?

How will you grab your reader's attention?

How will you state what the event is?

BODY

First Event	Second Event	Third Event
Details	Details	Details

CONCLUSION

What feelings or questions do you have about what you have observed?

What is the importance of the event?

What closing for the letter will you use?

NAME ______ CLASS ______ DATE ______

for **CHAPTER 20: YOUR TURN 8** *page 524*

Revising: Eyewitness Account

DIRECTIONS Use this chart to help you improve your eyewitness account.

QUESTIONS	DO THIS	CHANGES YOU MADE
1. Does the introduction grab the reader's attention?	☐ **Underline** the personal note, question, or story you used as the hook.	
2. Does the account provide background material and define unfamiliar terms and ideas for your reader?	☐ **Put stars** next to unfamiliar terms. ☐ **Circle** information that will help your reader understand them.	
3. Are the events in chronological order?	☐ **Number** each event, and check that the numbers match the order in which the events happened.	
4. Are there enough details to make the experience real?	☐ **Highlight** details and vivid descriptions to make the experience real for your reader.	
5. Does the conclusion show why the experience was important?	☐ **Put a check mark** next to statements explaining the importance of the event.	

NAME ______________________ CLASS ______________ DATE ______________

Revising Practice: Eyewitness Account

DIRECTIONS Below is an early draft of an eyewitness account.

- Revise the account to make it more effective, using the guidelines on page 522.
- Look for problems with the opening, background information, order, details, and conclusion.

Going to the nature preserve was interesting. My science class went to learn about local birds and wildlife. The first thing we did was go to a place for an orientation. A ranger said that we should not feed or touch the birds or animals.

In the preserve, we saw a falcon that had suffered a broken wing. Before that, we had seen two owls that had been wounded by a car. Finally, we saw a North American, or bald, eagle. It was majestic but had lost one of its wings in a forest fire when it was young.

We learned a lot from our trip to the nature preserve.

NAME ____________________ CLASS ____________ DATE ____________

Revising: Evaluating Eyewitness Accounts

DIRECTIONS Use the following questions to evaluate your eyewitness account or that of one of your classmates.

- Answer the questions.
- Rate the parts of the account. The lowest score is 1, and the highest is 4.
- Make at least three suggestions for improving the account.

1. How does the introduction grab the reader's attention?	**Rating** 1 2 3 4 ***Suggestion:***
2. What background information and definitions of unfamiliar terms and ideas does the account provide?	**Rating** 1 2 3 4 ***Suggestion:***
3. How closely do the events follow chronological order?	**Rating** 1 2 3 4 ***Suggestion:***
4. In what ways are details used to make the experience real for the reader?	**Rating** 1 2 3 4 ***Suggestion:***
5. How does the conclusion show that the experience was important?	**Rating** 1 2 3 4 ***Suggestion:***

Precise Nouns and Adjectives

DIRECTIONS Revise each of the passages below by replacing the vague nouns and adjectives with precise nouns and adjectives.

- First, underline the vague words and phrases. Then, above them, write precise words to replace them.
- After you have completed this exercise, revise your eyewitness account by replacing vague nouns and adjectives as directed in **Your Turn 8.**

PASSAGE A My friends and I went with my parents into the city. We visited the theater and saw a good show. People dressed in costumes sang songs about stuff. It was interesting when the actors came out after it. They looked completely different in their regular clothes.

PASSAGE B There was a fire at a school the other day. The kids were gone because it was vacation. Some firefighters came in a couple of fire trucks and put out the fire. People were happy about the situation. Apparently, some stuff caught fire in a room. It was a good thing that the school had smoke alarms.

PASSAGE C My dad and I had been planning this camping trip all year. We hiked down the beach a few miles and camped out. It would be great to wake up to the sun rising over the big ocean. The loud seagulls would probably want to share our good breakfast.

That night the wind died and the awful mosquitoes moved in. We tried everything to escape. My dad put on the cap he had packed in case his head got cold. I dug deep inside my sleeping bag. Neither of us will ever forget that bad night.

As we trudged over the sand dunes the next morning, we met a man heading toward the beach. Our sad faces told the sorry story. "No one told you?" he said. "This stretch of beach is called Mosquito Heaven."

NAME ____________________ CLASS ____________ DATE ____________

Proofreading: Punctuating Dialogue

DIRECTIONS Proofread and revise the following passage by correcting the mistakes in dialogue punctuation.

- Correct the errors by inserting the correct punctuation in or above the lines.
- After you have completed this exercise, proofread your eyewitness account for errors in dialogue punctuation, as directed in **Your Turn 9.**

A Saturday with Didi

In one year said Mr. Goldman the average American teenager sees more than twenty thousand commercials. Twenty thousand! And what do those commercials make you want to do?

We thought for a moment, and then someone raised a hand and said Buy stuff. Mr. Goldman nodded his head in agreement.

I decided to watch television one Saturday morning with my neighbor Didi, who is seven. I like programs about animals that talk Didi told me, so we watched a show about a pink talking elephant. The show was predictable, so mostly I watched Didi watch television. She laughed at all the jokes, but her eyes lit up like fireworks when the commercials came on. The ad for a talking doll made her say Wow! The one for the sugary sweet cereal prompted her to comment I like that stuff. It makes the milk turn blue.

During an hour of television, there were seventeen commercials. Four were for other television shows, five were for cereals or food, and eight were for toys.

I asked Didi Do you think television is a good thing?

Her answer was Yes. How else do you know what you want?

NAME CLASS DATE

for **CHAPTER 21: PREVIEW** **page 535**

Journal Warm-up: Instructions

Fruit smoothies make great after-school snacks. In a blender, mix one cup of milk with a cup of sliced banana or other fruit. Add three ice cubes and turn on the blender. Pour into a tall glass and enjoy!

Organizing a car wash for your club requires only three easy steps. First, locate a site and get permission to hold the car wash there. Advertise the event with radio announcements and posters placed in high-traffic areas. Arrive at the site with your own bucket, sponges, and clean towels.

JOURNAL STARTERS

Write for five minutes about how to do something, using one of these prompts.

- Explain how to play a sport or game you like.
- Write the directions from your school to your home.
- Describe the steps you follow to do something on your computer.
- Explain how to start a club at school.
- Describe how to operate a particular machine or device.

NAME ______________________ CLASS ______________ DATE ______________

for **CHAPTER 21: YOUR TURN 4** *page 546*

Prewriting: Choosing and Evaluating a Topic

DIRECTIONS Complete the following chart to help you choose a topic to write about.

- In the first column, list possible topics for your instructions.
- Evaluate your possible topics by completing the chart with comments on each question.
- Put a check mark next to the topic that is something you know how to do well and find interesting.

TOPIC	Is it something I do or make?	Can I do it? How well?	Is it interesting or unusual?

NAME ______________ CLASS ______________ DATE ______________

Prewriting: Your Audience and Purpose

DIRECTIONS Complete this chart to get a clearer picture of your audience and purpose.

QUESTIONS	ANSWERS
Who is my audience?	
What is my purpose?	
What special words or names go with my topic?	
How can I make the meaning of these words clear to a beginner?	
What parts of this activity are easier to show than to tell?	
What parts or special words of this activity are difficult to explain?	
How can I make these parts of the activity more clear to my audience?	

NAME ______________________ CLASS ______________ DATE ______________

for **CHAPTER 21: YOUR TURN 6** ***page 549***

Prewriting: Planning Your Instructions

DIRECTIONS Complete the steps below to help you gather and organize information about your activity.

- Make a list of the materials your activity requires.
- Make a list of the steps in your activity. Put the steps in chronological order by writing numbers next to them.
- Check for steps you may have left out, and add them. Renumber your steps if necessary.
- On a separate sheet of paper, create a flowchart of the activity.

Activity:

Materials:

____

____

____

____

____

____

____

____

____

____

____

____

STEP

↓

STEP

↓

STEP

↓

STEP

NAME ____________________ CLASS ____________ DATE ____________

for **INSTRUCTIONS** ***page 550***

Writing: Writing Prompts

DIRECTIONS Choose your own topic for your instructions, or use one of the following prompts.

SCHOOL

One of your classmates uses American Sign Language to communicate. You think it would be great if you and your classmates could learn sign language so that you could communicate directly with the student. How would you go about getting a sign language class started at your school? Talk to teachers or the principal about your idea. Then, write instructions for getting a class started.

WORKPLACE

School has just started, but you are already thinking about the job you want next summer at the community center. Although it is a volunteer job, many students apply and there is a lengthy interview process. Ask for tips from friends and relatives who have experience with interviews. Check out a library book or video about the process of interviewing. Write instructions for successfully completing an interview.

HEALTH AND SAFETY

On your way home from school one day, you notice that many students ignore traffic lights or cross where there are no crosswalks. You are concerned about their safety. Write instructions for designing an effective campaign to educate students about pedestrian safety.

TECHNOLOGY

A local television station is holding a contest for best educational video. The video must be about some aspect of life at your school. Think of a topic and how you would present it on video. Then, list the materials you would need and the steps you would take to produce the video. Ask a teacher or someone you know who is familiar with video technology to review your plan. Then, write it as a set of instructions for making a video.

MATHEMATICS

You have agreed to tutor a fifth-grade student in math. You meet with the student, who is bright and does well in class but has trouble solving problems on tests. Prepare a set of instructions that will help this student approach math problems in a test situation.

NAME CLASS DATE

for **CHAPTER 21: YOUR TURN 7** *page 550*

Writing: Drafting Your Instructions

DIRECTIONS Outline your paper or make notes, using the following organizer. After you have completed the organizer below, use it to write your first draft as instructed in **Your Turn 7.**

INTRODUCTION

▶ Interesting opening:

▶ Statement of topic:

▶ Reason for learning:

BODY

▶ Materials:

▶ **STEP 1** explanation (with relevant details):

▶ **STEP 2** explanation (with relevant details):

▶ **STEP 3** explanation (with relevant details):

CONCLUSION

▶ Restatement of reason for learning:

▶ Advice for doing activity or process:

Relevant and Irrelevant Details

DIRECTIONS The following instructions explain how to start a housesitting business. Each sentence is followed by a pair of brackets. Write *R* in the brackets if the sentence contains a *relevant* detail. Write *I* if it contains an *irrelevant* detail.

One way to earn money in the summer is to take care of plants or pets for neighbors who are on vacation. [ ] I housesat when my neighbors went hiking in the Rocky Mountains for two weeks last summer. [ ] Before your neighbors leave, visit their home and make notes about the plants or animals that will need your care. [ ] Some plants may not need to be watered every day. [ ] For example, cactuses need water only occasionally. [ ] I don't like cats, so I won't take jobs from people who have them. [ ] Also, talk to your neighbors about how frequently you should visit while they are gone. [ ] Don't be afraid to charge a little more money if you have to visit more than once a day. [ ] A pet-sitter once charged my family seven dollars per visit to check our dog. [ ] Finally, arrange a time to pick up a spare key, and make sure that it works—you don't want to be locked out of a job! [ ]

NAME ____________________ CLASS ____________ DATE ____________

for **CHAPTER 21: YOUR TURN 8** *page 557*

Revising: Instructions

DIRECTIONS Use this chart to help you improve your instructions.

QUESTIONS	DO THIS	CHANGES YOU MADE
1. Does the introduction clearly identify the activity or process?	☐ **Put a star** next to the statement that identifies the activity or process.	
2. Does the introduction give the reader a reason to learn the activity or process?	☐ **Underline** the reason for learning the activity or process.	
3. Do the steps show a logical progression of ideas?	☐ **Number** the steps.	
4. Do any steps need additional explanation?	☐ **Highlight** the explanation that follows each step.	
5. Are all details relevant to the instructions?	☐ **Write** an *R* by relevant details and an *I* by irrelevant ones.	
6. Does the conclusion restate the reason for learning the process and end with advice?	☐ **Put a check mark** next to the restatement. ☐ **Underline** the advice with a wavy line.	

NAME ______ CLASS ______ DATE ______

for **CHAPTER 21: YOUR TURN 8** *page 557*

Revising Practice: Instructions

DIRECTIONS Below is an early draft of a set of instructions.

- Revise the instructions to make them more effective, using the guidelines on page 555.
- Look for problems with the introduction, the order of steps, and the conclusion.

Yard clippings and leaves also make good composting material. Toss in any vegetable or fruit scraps, but no meat or dairy products, which will attract animals. To get started, use a wooden box or a purchased composting container. Occasionally add some water to keep the pile moist. Toss the pile with a pitchfork to make the compost turn more quickly. When you can feel the heat coming from the compost pile, you know the garbage is decaying. Sometimes you can even see steam rising. In five to seven months, when the compost material looks like soil, add it to your garden. Dig it into the soil and mix well.

NAME ____________ CLASS ____________ DATE ____________

Revising: Evaluating Instructions

DIRECTIONS Use the following questions to evaluate your instructions or that of one of your classmates.

- Answer the questions.
- Rate the parts of the instructions. The lowest score is 1, and the highest is 4.
- Make at least three suggestions for improving the instructions.

1. How clearly does the introduction state what the activity or process is?	**Rating** 1 2 3 4 ***Suggestion:***
2. How does the introduction interest the reader in learning the activity or process?	**Rating** 1 2 3 4 ***Suggestion:***
3. How clear is the sequence of steps?	**Rating** 1 2 3 4 ***Suggestion:***
4. How well are the steps explained?	**Rating** 1 2 3 4 ***Suggestion:***
5. Are any details not relevant? If so, which ones?	**Rating** 1 2 3 4 ***Suggestion:***
6. How well does the conclusion restate the reason for learning this process and give additional advice?	**Rating** 1 2 3 4 ***Suggestion:***

NAME CLASS DATE

Prepositional Phrases

DIRECTIONS Revise the following passages by adding prepositional phrases as transitions.

- Choose prepositions from the list below.
- Add prepositional phrases to the passages to connect ideas and improve the instructions.
- After you have completed this exercise, revise your instructions by adding transitional prepositional phrases as directed in **Your Turn 8.**

about	from	on
after	in	to
at	inside	under
before	near	until
during	of	with

PASSAGE A Exercising is good for you. Do some stretching to warm your muscles. Start slowly. Find a comfortable pace. Increase your pace only when you feel ready. Relax your mind, but pay attention. When you are tired, slow down. Stretch again to cool your muscles.

PASSAGE B A scrapbook is a good place to keep your memories. It is a good idea to arrange your "scraps." Lay out your photos and other keepsakes. Try several different arrangements. When you find the layout you like best, use a little paste or glue. Next, place the item flat and smooth it down. Leave room to write captions. Write your name and the date.

Proofreading: Introductory Prepositional Phrases

DIRECTIONS Proofread the following passages, and decide if each of the underlined introductory prepositional phrases should have a comma after it.

- If a comma is needed, insert it in the correct place. If a comma is not needed, write C above the phrase.
- After you have completed this exercise, proofread and correct your "how-to" paper as directed in **Your Turn 9.**

PASSAGE A Practicing a family fire drill could save a life. With an adult plan the exits each person will use. For an emergency decide on alternative escape routes and a definite place to meet outside. Review what to do if clothing catches fire—stop, drop, and roll. After agreeing on procedures run through a fire drill. At the end of the drill check with each other to see what might not have worked. During a real fire everyone will know what to do.

PASSAGE B In our community theater production of *The Wizard of Oz* I play the role of the Cowardly Lion. For this role applying makeup can be a long process. To my clean face I apply greasepaint with my fingertips, blending it carefully. Under my eyes I add darker makeup to make shadows. I make the wrinkles on my forehead with brown pencils. On my cheeks I apply two circles of rouge and add lipstick. I lightly powder my face to set the makeup. Then, the makeup artist applies my whiskers with a special glue called spirit gum. Looking both very fierce and very sad, I am ready to walk onstage and roar.

NAME ____________________ CLASS ____________ DATE ____________

Explaining "How-to" for Tests

DIRECTIONS Complete the following steps to help you understand "how-to" writing prompts.

- Choose one of the writing prompts below.
- Complete the graphic organizer for the writing prompt you chose.
- Study your brainstorming notes, and write your "how-to" paper.
- Re-read your paper, adding details and explanations as needed.

PROMPTS

- You are part of a committee planning to create a photo album or a scrapbook of your community for a centennial celebration. Write a memo to the local historical society explaining the steps of your plan.
- Students have different approaches to studying for a test. Some strategies are more successful than others. Think about your most successful strategy for studying for a test. Then, explain your strategy to other students.
- You have watched your grandmother make your favorite meal many times. Now you are going to stay at a friend's house, and you would like to make that meal. Think of the ingredients and steps involved in making the meal. Write the recipe.
- Your younger brother is interested in playing the same musical instrument that you play. Explain the steps he needs to follow in order to learn to play the instrument.

STEP 1: Study the prompt.

Purpose: ____________________

Audience: ____________________

Form of "how-to" paper: ____________________

STEP 2: Decide on topic of "how-to" paper.

STEP 3:

Brainstorm steps.	**Determine the order of steps.**

Journal Warm-up: Advantages/Disadvantages

I was so excited to hear that our new apartment complex allows pets. I've always wanted a cat; they're quiet and easy to care for. I'll have to clean more often because of the cat hair, though, and I really dislike cleaning.

"What a great trail!" Luis exclaimed, looking at the rushing river below. Cody crawled to the cliff's edge. "Yes," he replied, "but the last mile was straight up, and I hate heights."

JOURNAL STARTERS

Write about advantages and disadvantages for five minutes, using one of these prompts.

- Discuss the pros and cons of bringing your lunch to school.
- What are the good and bad things about being on a sports team?
- Explain the advantages and disadvantages of living in a large city or small town.
- Explain the pros and cons of being the oldest, youngest, middle, or only child in your family.
- Write about the good and bad things about doing volunteer work after school.

NAME ____________________ CLASS ____________ DATE ____________

for **CHAPTER 22: YOUR TURN 4** *page 579*

Prewriting: Possible Topics and Audience

DIRECTIONS Use the graphic organizer below to evaluate topics for your advantages/disadvantages essay and to help you understand your audience.

- Jot down at least three advantages and three disadvantages for each topic.

CHOOSE A TOPIC

Topic A:	**Topic B:**	**Topic C:**
Advantages:	Advantages:	Advantages:
Disadvantages:	Disadvantages:	Disadvantages:

Best topic:

IDENTIFY YOUR AUDIENCE

Who will need information about my topic?	
What will this audience need to know to get a balanced picture of the advantages and disadvantages of my topic?	
What does this audience already know about my topic?	

NAME ______________________ CLASS ______________ DATE ______________

for **CHAPTER 22: YOUR TURN 5** ***page 580***

Prewriting: Listing Advantages and Disadvantages

DIRECTIONS Use the fishbone organizer to list all the advantages and disadvantages you can think of that relate to your topic.

- Write the advantages on the lines to the left and the disadvantages on the lines to the right.
- Make sure you have at least three advantages and three disadvantages. If you have more, add lines as needed.

Topic: ____

Advantages | Disadvantages

NAME ____________ CLASS ____________ DATE ____________

Prewriting: Choosing Advantages and Disadvantages

DIRECTIONS Use the concept map below to decide which advantages and disadvantages to write about in your essay.

- Write the topic of your essay at the top of the map.
- List each advantage and disadvantage.
- Add support for each advantage and disadvantage.
- Note whether each piece of support is a fact (*F*), expert opinion (*EO*), or anecdote (*A*).
- After filling in the map, cross out any advantage or disadvantage you could not support.

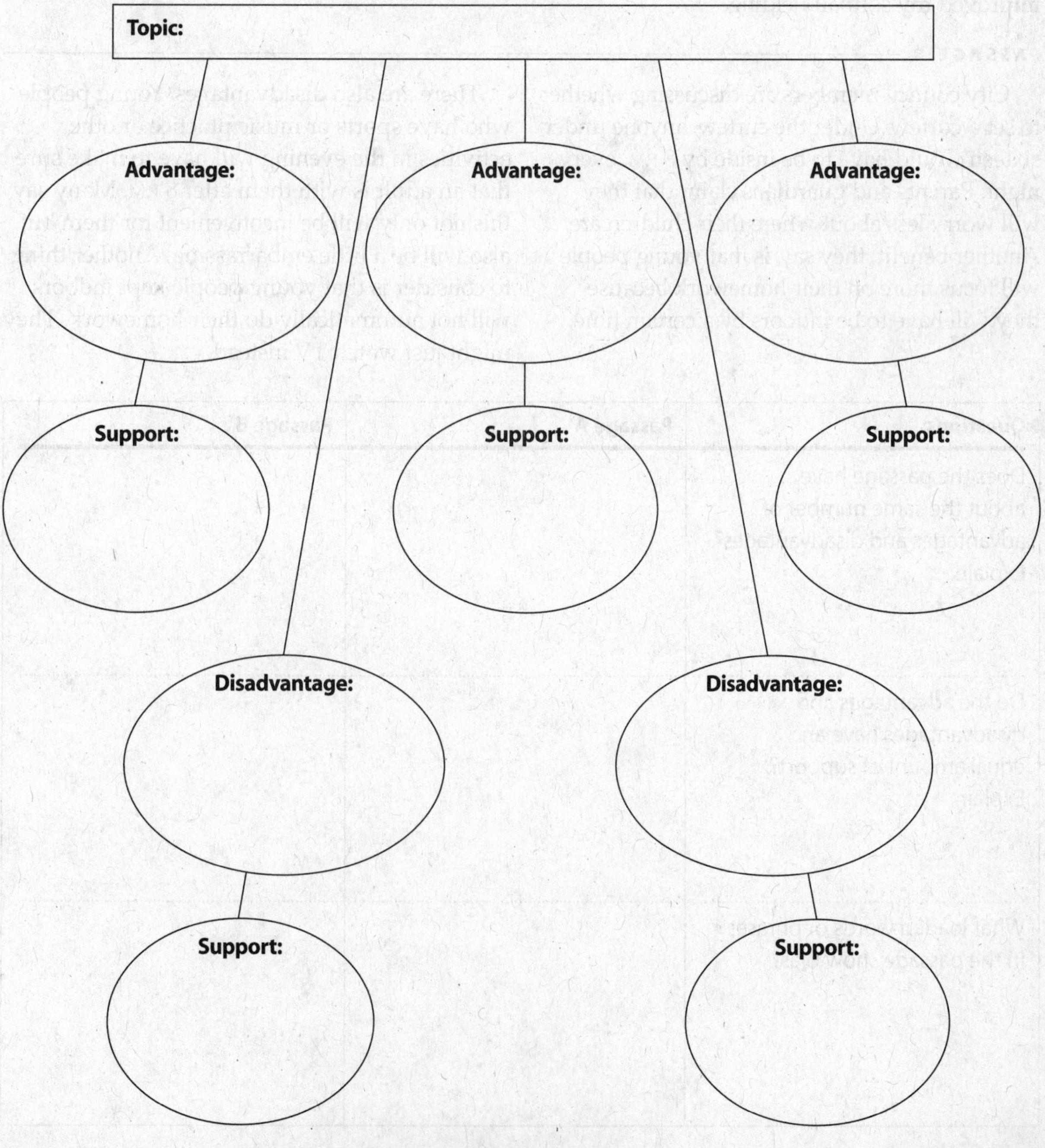

NAME _______________ CLASS _______________ DATE _______________

Telling the Difference Between Balance and Bias

DIRECTIONS Use the chart to identify balance and bias in the passages below.

PASSAGE A

People think that video games are bad for young people, but I disagree. One advantage of video games is that they keep you very alert. If you lose focus for even a second, you can lose the game. Also, video games are great for developing eye-hand coordination. I am totally convinced that playing video games has improved my softball fielding.

Of course, young people spend too much time playing video games, time they could spend on homework, chores, or other things. Young people who are constantly playing video games make it hard for the rest of us to enjoy a game once in a while.

PASSAGE B

City council members are discussing whether to set a curfew. Under the curfew, anyone under sixteen would have to be inside by 8 P.M. every night. Parents and guardians claim that they will worry less about where their children are. Another benefit, they say, is that young people will focus more on their homework because they will have to be indoors by a certain time.

There are also disadvantages. Young people who have sports or music practice or other activities in the evening will have to make sure that an adult is with them after 8 P.M. Many say this not only will be inconvenient for them but also will be a little embarrassing. Another thing to consider is that young people kept indoors will not automatically do their homework. They might just watch TV instead.

Questions	Passage A	Passage B
Does the passage have about the same number of advantages and disadvantages? Explain.		
Do the advantages and disadvantages have an equal amount of support? Explain.		
What loaded words or phrases in the passage show bias?		

NAME ______ CLASS ______ DATE ______

for **CHAPTER 22: YOUR TURN 7** ***page 583***

Prewriting: Organizing Your Essay

DIRECTIONS Use the graphic organizers and questions below to help you organize your essay.

- Jot down your two advantages and two disadvantages.
- Answer the questions about the order of your essay.
- Fill in the outline at the bottom of the page to show the order of advantages and disadvantages in your essay.

Advantage:

Advantage:

Disadvantage:

Disadvantage:

- Will I discuss advantages or disadvantages first? Why?

ORDER OF MY ESSAY

Advantages	**Disadvantages**
1.	**1.**
2.	**2.**
3.	**3.**

- Why is this a good order?

NAME ______ CLASS ______ DATE ______

for **ADVANTAGES/DISADVANTAGES ESSAY** **page 577**

Writing: Writing Prompts

DIRECTIONS Choose your own topic for your advantages/disadvantages essay, or use one of the following prompts.

WORKPLACE
Your parents have offered to pay you to watch your younger brother for three hours every afternoon. Some afternoons, though, you and your friends like to go swimming at the community pool. Write to your parents explaining the advantages and disadvantages of taking the job.

SCHOOL
Your school has recently received some money from a local company. There are many ways that the money could be spent—the science lab needs new microscopes, the computer lab is out-of-date, and the track needs to be repaired. Choose one of the three ways the money should be spent. Then write to your school board explaining the advantages and disadvantages of your choice.

LANGUAGES
Students at your school begin studying a new language in seventh grade. Your school offers French, German, and Spanish. You want to study Spanish. After exploring the advantages and disadvantages of learning Spanish, write to your guidance counselor explaining your choice.

SCIENCE
Your science teacher has asked your class to form into groups, and for each group to prepare a presentation. Write a list of the advantages and disadvantages of working in groups. Then, write to the other members of your group explaining how you feel about working in groups.

PHYSICAL EDUCATION
Every six weeks in gym class, students sign up to learn more about different activities. For this period your choices are basketball, weight training, or aerobics. Choose one of the activities and list the advantages and disadvantages of learning the activity. Then, write a statement explaining which activity you chose and why.

NAME ______ CLASS ______ DATE ______

for **CHAPTER 22: YOUR TURN 8** *page 584*

Writing: Advantages/Disadvantages Essay

DIRECTIONS Use the following organizer to outline your essay or make notes.

- After you have completed the organizer, use it to help you write your first draft as instructed in **Your Turn 8.**

INTRODUCTION

▶ How will you grab your audience's attention?

▶ What is your main idea?

BODY

▶ **First Paragraph**	▶ **Second Paragraph**
What is your first advantage/disadvantage?	What is your second advantage/disadvantage?
How will you support it?	How will you support it?
▶ **Third Paragraph**	▶ **Fourth Paragraph**
What is your third disadvantage/advantage?	What is your fourth disadvantage/advantage?
How will you support it?	How will you support it?

CONCLUSION

▶ How will you restate an advantage and a disadvantage?

NAME ____________ CLASS ____________ DATE ____________

for **CHAPTER 22: YOUR TURN 9** ***page 590***

Revising: Advantages/Disadvantages Essay

DIRECTIONS: Use this chart to help you improve your advantages/disadvantages essay.

QUESTIONS	DO THIS	CHANGES YOU MADE
1. Does the introduction include a main idea statement?	☐ **Circle** the main idea statement.	
2. Are all advantages and all disadvantages grouped together?	☐ **Put a star** next to each advantage and a **check mark** next to each disadvantage.	
3. Is each advantage and disadvantage explained and supported?	☐ **Highlight** the explanation and support for each advantage and disadvantage.	
4. Does the conclusion restate both an advantage and a disadvantage?	☐ **Bracket** the restated advantage and disadvantage.	
5. Does the essay present a balanced discussion of the topic?	☐ **Put exclamation points** next to opinions and biased words. ☐ **Count** the advantages and disadvantages.	

NAME ______________________ CLASS ______________ DATE ______________

Revising Practice: Advantages/Disadvantages

DIRECTIONS Below is an early draft of an advantages/disadvantages essay.

- Revise the essay to make it more effective, using the guidelines on page 588.
- Look for problems with the main idea statement, grouping advantages and disadvantages together, support for each advantage and disadvantage, and balance.

My sisters and I had finished cleaning the basement, our Saturday chore. We had several piles of items we no longer used or wanted—crayons, old board games, and clothing we had outgrown. I thought we would simply fill up trash bags and head for the dumpster.

"Why not have a garage sale instead?" suggested my older sister. "We could each sell the items we no longer want. It would be fun."

I thought the idea was stupid and said so. A garage sale meant more work and would be a waste of time.

"It would be better for the environment," my younger sister pointed out.

NAME CLASS DATE

for CHAPTER 22: YOUR TURN 9 **page 590** PEER- AND SELF-EVALUATION FORM

Revising: Advantages/Disadvantages Essays

DIRECTIONS Use the following questions to evaluate your advantages/disadvantages essay or that of one of your classmates.

- Answer the questions.
- Rate the parts of the essay. The lowest score is 1, and the highest is 4.
- Make at least three suggestions for improving the essay.

1. How does the introduction grab readers' attention?	**Rating** 1 2 3 4 ***Suggestion:***
2. What main idea is stated in the introduction?	**Rating** 1 2 3 4 ***Suggestion:***
3. How are the advantages and disadvantages grouped together?	**Rating** 1 2 3 4 ***Suggestion:***
4. Is each advantage and disadvantage explained and supported well?	**Rating** 1 2 3 4 ***Suggestion:***
5. What advantage and disadvantage are restated?	**Rating** 1 2 3 4 ***Suggestion:***
6. Is the essay's discussion of the topic well-balanced?	**Rating** 1 2 3 4 ***Suggestion:***

NAME ______________________ CLASS ____________ DATE ____________

Stringy Sentences

DIRECTIONS Fix the stringy sentences by breaking them into separate sentences.

- Insert the correct punctuation. Cross out words that are not needed in the revised sentences and add words that are needed.
- After you have completed the exercise, revise your advantages/disadvantages essay, correcting any stringy sentences as directed in **Your Turn 9.**

1. Sometimes we get so busy that we grab supper at the drive-through but I am happiest when we are all home and then we make a real meal together.

2. We used to live in Florida where it was always summer and I could go to the beach every day but now we live in Michigan and I am learning to enjoy winter sports.

3. My friends and I like to go fishing but it is hard to get up early in the summer but we manage to do it at least once a week and we ride our bikes to the lake and we always catch a few fish but we usually throw them back because they are small.

4. Vanessa volunteered to work in a soup kitchen and she discovered that feeding hungry people is a lot of work but she did not mind because she enjoys cooking and helping others and she even got some of her friends to help.

5. The animal shelter is full of dogs and they need good homes but many of the dogs have not had any training and they need at least some training before people will adopt them but luckily a local dog-obedience instructor offered to train the dogs for free.

NAME ______________________ CLASS ______________ DATE ______________

for **GRAMMAR LINK** ***page 591*** **ADDITIONAL PRACTICE**

Proofreading: Correcting Run-ons

DIRECTIONS Locate and revise run-on sentences in the following passages.

- If a sentence is a run-on, revise it by inserting a semicolon or a comma and a conjunction in the correct place.
- If a sentence is not a run-on, write C following the sentence.
- After you have completed this exercise, proofread and correct your advantages/disadvantages essay as directed in **Your Turn 10.**

PASSAGE A Finding research material on the Internet has made it easier for me to do research papers I do not have to drag home a lot of books from the library to find good information. I have to check the sources I use more carefully it is important that they be reliable. I usually look for Internet sites from museums, educational institutions, or government agencies I never use information from a personal Web site. One disadvantage to using Internet sources is that I tend to wait until the last minute to start a paper then if I really cannot find anything, I don't have time to go to the library. I simply need to discipline myself to start my research early and to use the resources wisely. I could check out the library's resources first then I could add online resources.

PASSAGE B This year I am finally able to go to band camp this is something I have wanted to do for a long time. I enjoy spending the summers playing with my friends this will be a real chance to improve my trumpet-playing skills. My sister went to camp last year I was amazed at the difference it made. Holding a sticky trumpet in 90-degree weather with sweat rolling off my face does not sound like much fun. I know, however, that I will make new friends at band camp my sister did. I have begun saving money already after all, camp is not free.

NAME ______________________ CLASS ______________ DATE ______________

for **TEST-TAKING MINI-LESSON** ***page 593*** **PRACTICE**

Explaining Advantages and Disadvantages for Tests

DIRECTIONS On a separate sheet of paper, copy and complete the graphic organizer below for each of the four prompts.

- Then, respond to one of the prompts in writing.
- Make sure you have supported each good and bad point. Finally, check your essay for correct grammar and spelling.

PROMPTS

- The school district is planning to close all the small middle schools in your community and open one big one. This would mean many changes. For example, classes would be bigger, and some students would have to ride buses to school. Identify the advantages and disadvantages of such a plan in an essay for members of the school community.
- One of your parents has just gotten a new job in another country. This means that you must move to a place where you do not know anyone or even speak the language. In a short essay, share with a parent some of the advantages and disadvantages of such a move.
- You have always enjoyed singing, and your teachers think that you are gifted. They have suggested that you attend a high school for the performing arts. This would mean leaving your friends and getting serious about singing. Examine the advantages and disadvantages of such a decision in a short essay to a friend.
- Your older brother has just left home to go to college. For the first time, you will have your own room and won't have to share space with him. Write a short essay for your brother about the advantages and disadvantages of having your own room.

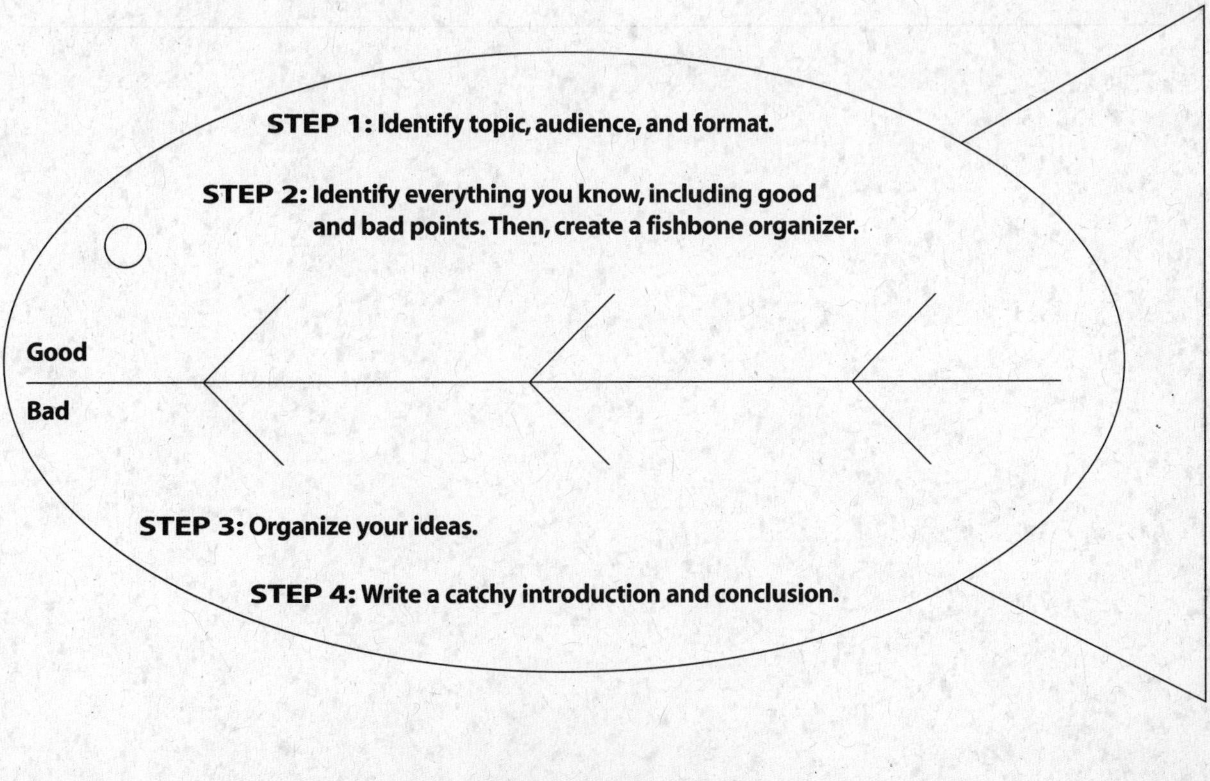

Journal Warm-up: Book Jacket

I love browsing in the science fiction section of the bookstore. The book jackets, especially the covers, are so amazing! They also help me quickly find a good book.

I've found a new book on Web searches that seems to be just what I need. According to the jacket, the book has clear instructions, helpful illustrations, and a reader-friendly tone. I can use all the help I can get in finding reliable information and sites on the Web.

JOURNAL STARTERS

Write for five minutes about previewing books, using one of these prompts.

- How would you choose a novel to read for a book report?
- Describe how you might find a book to give to a family member.
- How would you select a new book to review for your school's newspaper?
- Explain how you would find a book for a young child.
- Tell how you might choose one book among several by a writer you like.

NAME ____________________ CLASS __________ DATE __________

Prewriting: Selecting a Novel and an Audience

DIRECTIONS Complete the graphic organizer below to help you select a novel and target your audience.

SELECT A NOVEL

My favorite kinds of novels are about ______________________________ ______________________________ ______________________________.

The most exciting moment I remember from a novel is ______________________________ ______________________________ ______________________________.

I would be interested in reading or re-reading the following novel:

TARGET YOUR AUDIENCE

My primary audience will be young adults. They would be interested in ______________________________ ______________________________ ______________________________ ______________________________ ______________________________ ______________________________

My secondary audience will be parents and librarians. They would be interested in ______________________________ ______________________________ ______________________________ ______________________________ ______________________________ ______________________________

NAME ____________ CLASS ____________ DATE ____________

for **CHAPTER 23: YOUR TURN 5** ***page 618***

Prewriting: Selecting a Cover Image and a Quotation

DIRECTIONS Use the charts below to help you select an image for the front cover and a quotation for the back cover of your book jacket. Then, make a sketch of your front cover on a separate sheet of paper.

SELECTING A FRONT COVER IMAGE

Scene	Analysis	Rank

CHOOSING ELEMENTS FOR THE COVER IMAGE

Questions About Scene You Chose	Your Answers
Who or what is the major focus of the scene?	
What action takes place during the scene?	
What emotions or feelings are present in the scene?	
What is the setting of the scene? What does the place look like?	

SELECTING A QUOTATION

Important Moment	Possible Quotation	Rank

NAME ______ CLASS ______ DATE ______

Elements of Fiction

DIRECTIONS Use the organizer below to help you identify the characters, setting, plot, and theme of a novel or other story you have read.

STORY: ______

Characters:

Setting:

PLOT

Event 1:

Event 2:

Event 3:

Event 4:

Theme:

NAME ______ CLASS ______ DATE ______

for **CHAPTER 23: YOUR TURN 6** *page 621*

Prewriting: Writing the Front Flap

DIRECTIONS Use the charts below to help you gather information for your summary and front flap.

HOOK

What small bit of information would make the reader want to know more about the novel?	

SUMMARY

Characters: Who is the main character? What is he or she like? What is that character interested in or concerned about?	
Setting: Where does the story take place? Is it set in the past, present, or future?	
Plot: What major problem does the main character face? In general, how does he or she respond to that problem? (Be careful; do not give away too much of the plot.)	
Theme: What idea about life do you think the author is trying to give you? What does he or she want readers to learn from this novel?	

REASONS FOR READING

Why should people read this novel? What will they get out of it?	

NAME ______________________ CLASS ______________ DATE ______________

Prewriting: Researching the Author

DIRECTIONS Use a library or the Internet to help you search for information about the author of your novel. Use the organizer below to take notes on important or interesting details that you can use in creating your book jacket.

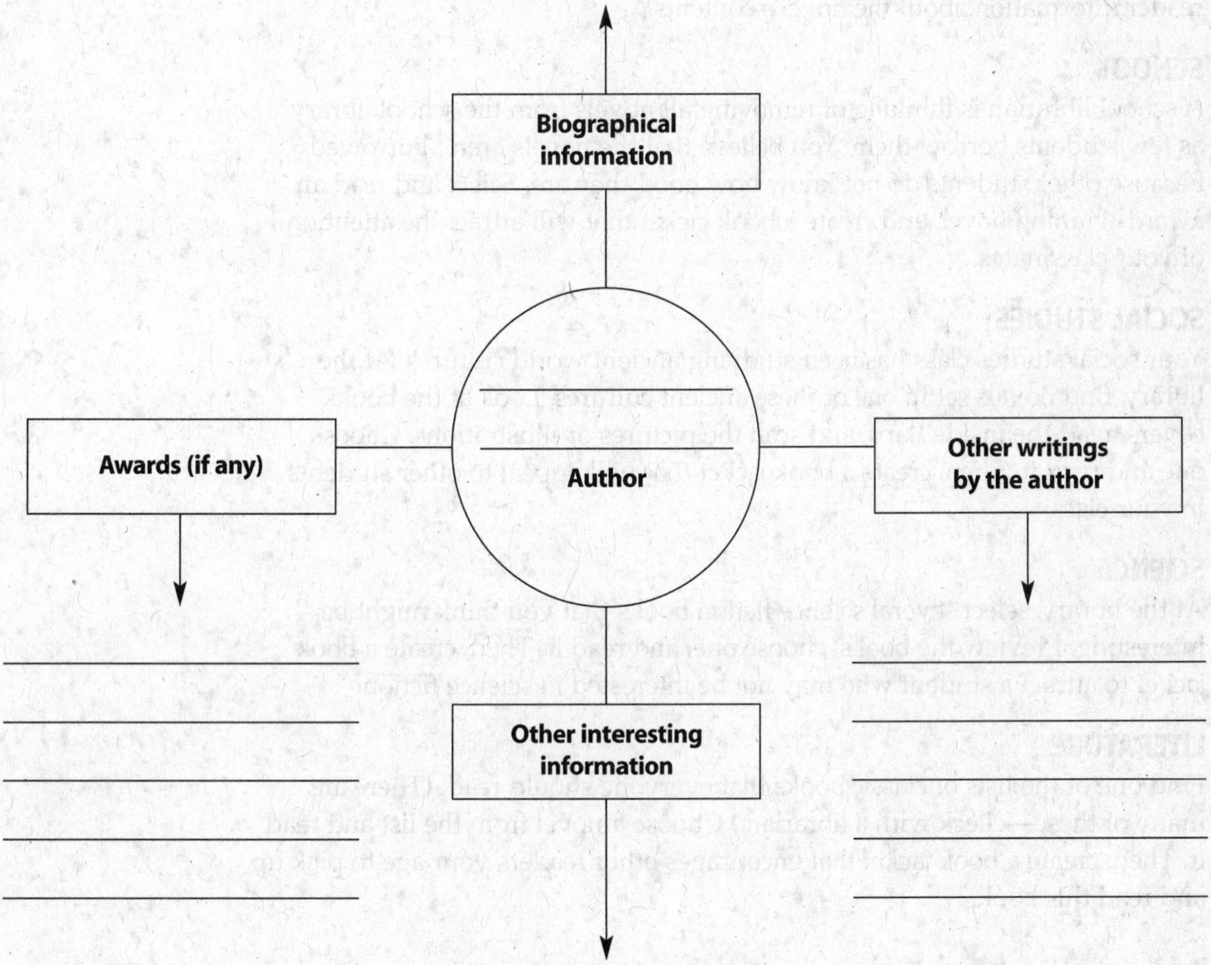

NAME ______________________ CLASS ______________ DATE ______________

for **BOOK JACKET** ***page 624***

Writing: Writing Prompts

DIRECTIONS Choose your own novel for your book jacket, or use one of the following prompts.

CAREERS

You love animals and have considered becoming a veterinarian. The vet who cares for your pets has recommended that you read some books about animals. At the library, select novels about animals. Preview the books. Choose one and read it. Then, create a book jacket that will give another reader information about the novel's contents.

SCHOOL

A school librarian is thinking of removing all novels from the school library as few students borrow them. You believe that the novels aren't borrowed because other students do not know how good they are. Select and read an award-winning novel, and create a book jacket that will attract the attention of your classmates.

SOCIAL STUDIES

Your social studies class has been studying ancient world cultures. At the library, find novels set in one of these ancient cultures. Look at the books' covers, read the inside flaps, and scan the pictures or illustrations. Choose one and read it. Then, create a book jacket that will appeal to other students in your class.

SCIENCE

At the library, select several science fiction books that you think might be interesting. Preview the books, choose one, and read it. Then, create a book jacket to attract a student who may not be interested in science fiction.

LITERATURE

Find one of the lists of classic books that everyone should read. (There are many of these—check with a librarian.) Choose a novel from the list and read it. Then, create a book jacket that encourages other readers your age to pick up and read this book.

NAME ____________________ CLASS ____________ DATE ____________

Writing: Drafting Your Book Jacket

DIRECTIONS Complete the graphic organizer below, and use it to help you write the first draft of your book jacket. Use additional paper if necessary.

FRONT COVER

▶ Who is the author and what is the title?

▶ What meaningful image will you use?

FRONT FLAP

▶ How will you hook the reader's attention?

▶ What is your summary and reason for reading the book?

BACK COVER

▶ What catchy quotation or passage will you include?

BACK FLAP

▶ What information about the author will you provide?

NAME ______________________ CLASS ______________ DATE ______________

for **CHAPTER 23: YOUR TURN 9** ***page 627***

Revising: Book Jacket

DIRECTIONS Use this chart to help you improve your book jacket.

QUESTIONS	DO THIS	CHANGES YOU MADE
1. Does the cover image grab the audience's attention?	☐ **Use sticky notes** to mark three things in the illustration that would interest readers.	
2. Does the front flap hook the reader?	☐ **Circle** the hook. If necessary, add a statement that will make readers want to read this novel.	
3. Does the summary include details about character, setting, plot, and theme?	☐ **Underline** the details. ☐ **Label** the element each describes. Add details if needed.	
4. Does the summary provide a reason for reading that will encourage people to read the novel?	☐ **Place a star** by the reason for reading. If the reason wouldn't make *you* want to read the novel, revise it.	
5. Does the back cover quotation make sense and make audiences want to read the novel?	☐ Ask a friend who has not read the novel to **evaluate the quotation.** If your friend doesn't find it interesting, pick a new one.	
6. Are interesting facts and details about the author included in the biography?	☐ **Highlight** the facts and details in the biography. Add more if these are not interesting.	

NAME ______________________ CLASS ______________ DATE ______________

Revising Practice: Book Jacket

DIRECTIONS Below is an early draft of a book jacket's front flap.

- Revise the book jacket to make it more effective, using the guidelines on page 625.
- Look for problems with the hook, details in the summary, and a reason for reading.

(Front Flap)

Ella Enchanted is a retelling of the Cinderella story. Although the plot is the same as the traditional fairy tale, Ella's ideas are contemporary. For example, she studies foreign languages and is interested in other cultures.

At her mother's funeral, Ella meets Prince Charmont, who also grieves. They become friends, sharing an interest in animals. Ella likes to use her wit to make the Prince laugh. However, Ella is sent away to boarding school with two hateful girls who will become her stepsisters. Ella runs away from boarding school and has many adventures. She finally attends the Prince's ball.

DATA

- Ella is a sassy, smart heroine.
- Ella solves her own problems.
- The setting is a kingdom that can't be found on any recent maps.
- The theme teaches lessons about love and doing one's best.
- This is an upbeat story of a clever, loyal girl who triumphs over misfortune.

NAME ____________ CLASS ____________ DATE ____________

for **CHAPTER 23: YOUR TURN 9** ***page 627*** **PEER- AND SELF-EVALUATION FORM**

Revising: Evaluating Book Jackets

DIRECTIONS Use the following questions to evaluate your book jacket or that of one of your classmates.

- Answer the questions.
- Rate the parts of the book jacket. The lowest score is 1, and the highest is 4.
- Make at least three suggestions for improving the book jacket.

1. How does the cover image grab the audience's attention?	**Rating** 1 2 3 4 ***Suggestion:***
2. How does the front flap hook the reader?	**Rating** 1 2 3 4 ***Suggestion:***
3. What kinds of details about character, setting, plot, and theme does the summary include?	**Rating** 1 2 3 4 ***Suggestion:***
4. What reason is given for reading the book?	**Rating** 1 2 3 4 ***Suggestion:***
5. What is interesting about the back cover quotation?	**Rating** 1 2 3 4 ***Suggestion:***
6. What interesting facts and details about the author are included in the biography?	**Rating** 1 2 3 4 ***Suggestion:***

NAME ______ CLASS ______ DATE ______

Combining Sentences

DIRECTIONS Revise the passages below by combining short, choppy sentences that are related.

- To create a compound sentence, place a comma after the first sentence and add a conjunction such as *and*, *but*, or *or*.
- After you have completed this exercise, revise your book jacket by combining any short, choppy sentences, as directed in **Your Turn 9.**

PASSAGE A *Tuck Everlasting*, by Natalie Babbitt, is a fantasy novel that tells the story of a lonely young girl, Winnie Foster. Winnie lives in a dusty little town called Treegap. She thinks about running away. She makes an exciting discovery in the forest one day. Winnie is kidnapped by the Tuck family. She learns the secret they are determined to protect from all outsiders. Handsome young Jesse Tuck determines to marry Winnie. He makes plans for a long future with her. Winnie is confused by all the attention from the Tuck family. In the end, she makes her own difficult decision.

PASSAGE B Georgia Hughes lives with her father in Brazil. Her mother lives in Washington, D. C. Georgia loves Brazil's tropical setting. Her parents send her to a girls' boarding school in Connecticut. Georgia feels her own father does not care about her. She pretends that John F. Kennedy, the president of the United States, is her father. She packs a photograph of Kennedy when she goes to boarding school. She spends her time writing letters to Kennedy. She does not mail them. *When JFK Was My Father* is an amusing story that has been nominated for an award. The author, Amy Gordon, also attended boarding school. She also lived in Brazil.

NAME ______________________ CLASS ______________ DATE ______________

for **GRAMMAR LINK** *page 628* **ADDITIONAL PRACTICE**

Proofreading: Hyphenation

DIRECTIONS Proofread the following passage from a book jacket.

- Correct the words that are incorrectly hyphenated.
- After you have completed this exercise, proofread your book jacket for errors in hyphenation as directed in **Your Turn 10**.

Tales to Tell

Once upon a time there were two bro-
thers, Jakob and Wilhelm Grimm. Their go-
al was to collect and record the fascinati-
ng folk tales they had been told as childr-
en. At the beginning of the nineteenth cent-
ury, many of these tales had never been wr-
itten down.

The brothers traveled across Germany, sear-
ching the countryside, asking elderly peasants
and townspeople to retell the tra-
ditional tales. Then the brothers publ-
ished the stories in a series of books, which
quickly became popular. The tales are still fav-
orites of children and adults alike.

However, many of these stories are not for
everyone, and parental guidance should be ex-
ercised. Although good generally wins over e-
vil, in the course of these tales, people are
killed and even eaten. Family members are ho-
rribly cruel to one another. Many experts belie-
ve that stories like these actually help childr-
en overcome their deepest fears.

Journal Warm-up: Informative Article

Quick, name an animal that builds towns! Native to the western United States, prairie dogs live underground in elaborate networks of burrows called towns. These towns house thousands of residents, have numerous entrances, and can cover an area of 160 acres.

"There was absolutely nothing to excite ambition for education," Abraham Lincoln said of growing up on the Indiana frontier. Yet with less than a year of formal education, Lincoln determined to educate himself. He walked long distances to borrow books, including law books. Eventually he joined a law practice in Springfield, Illinois.

Each spring millions of people lose an hour as Daylight Saving Time goes into effect. Each spring the question "why are we doing this?" has to be answered again.

JOURNAL STARTERS

Write for five minutes, using one of the prompts below.

- About what scientific invention would you like more information?
- What historical event interests you? What do you already know about it?
- What would you like to know about meteors or some other celestial body?
- Write about a holiday tradition with which you are familiar.
- Write about a famous person you find fascinating.

NAME ______________________ CLASS ______________ DATE ______________

Prewriting: Choosing and Focusing a Subject

DIRECTIONS Use the conceptual map below to choose a subject and focus.

- Write a subject in the center circle.
- Write specific topics related to the subject in the connecting circles.
- Make a check mark in the circle of the specific topic that is most interesting to you.

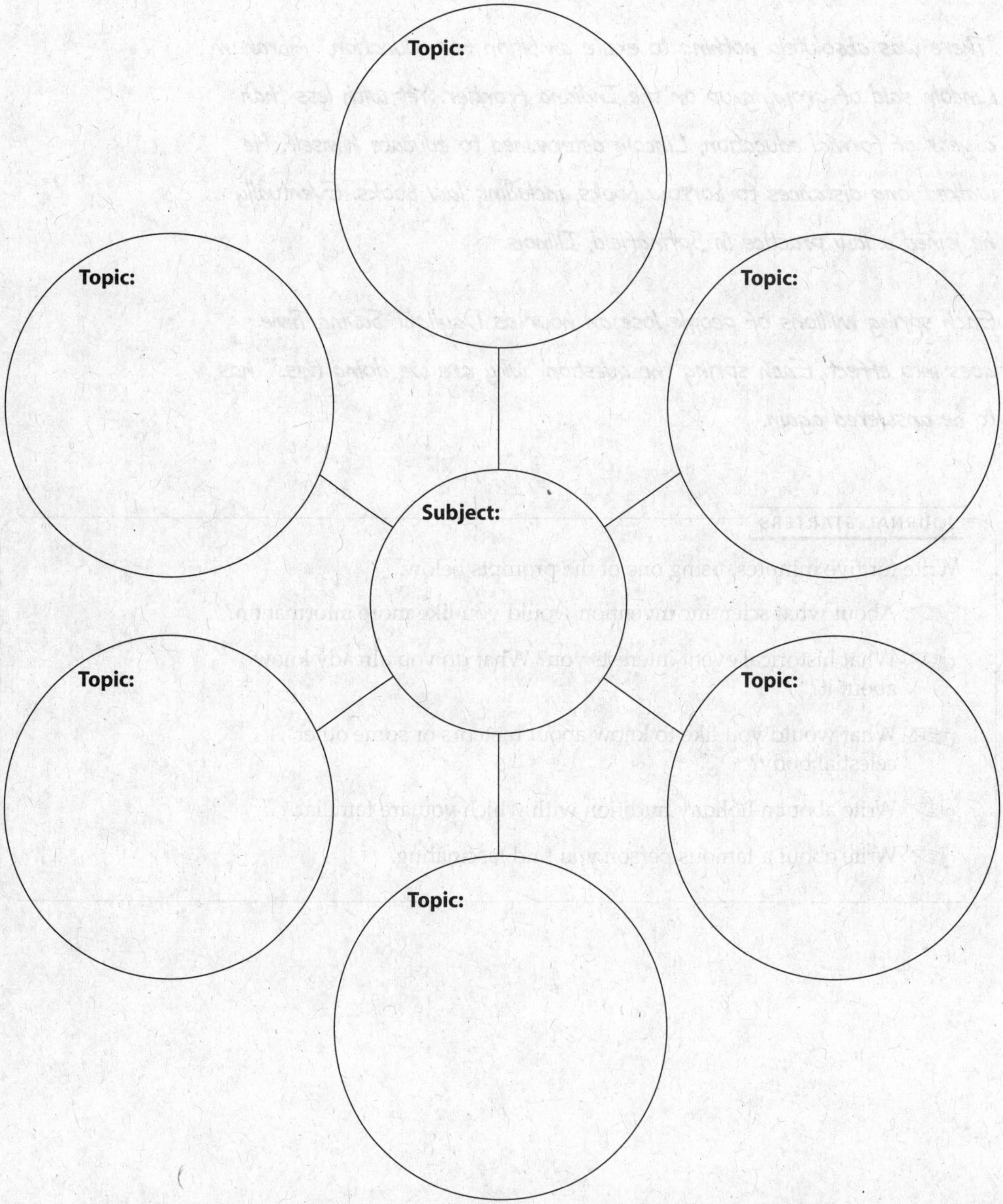

NAME CLASS DATE

for **CHAPTER 24: YOUR TURN 5** ***page 657***

Prewriting: Audience, Purpose, Asking Questions

DIRECTIONS Use the charts below to identify your audience and purpose.

- Answer the questions in the first chart to identify your audience's needs.
- In the second chart, list the information you already know about your topic and questions you still have about it. These questions are your research questions.

Question	Explanation
What do my readers already know about my topic?	
What do my readers need to know about my topic?	
What can they do with the information?	

What do I already know?

Research Questions

Who:

What:

Where:

When:

Why:

How:

NAME ______________________ CLASS ______________ DATE ______________

Prewriting: Find Sources and Make a Source List

DIRECTIONS Use this worksheet to help you create a source list.

- Check the different types of sources you have found for your report of information. Make sure you have at least three different types of sources.
- Make a source list in the space provided.

Types of Sources

____ Books	____ Magazine or Newspaper Articles
____ Electronic Sources	____ Movie or DVD Recordings
____ Encyclopedia Articles	____ Television or Radio Programs
____ Interviews	

Source List

1. ______________________________

2. ______________________________

3. ______________________________

4. ______________________________

5. ______________________________

6. ______________________________

7. ______________________________

8. ______________________________

9. ______________________________

NAME ____________ CLASS ____________ DATE ____________

Evaluating Sources

DIRECTIONS Below are ten descriptions of sources for a research paper on the effects of diabetes. Identify each description as either a preferred source or a less reliable source.

- If the source is preferred, write *P* in the space to the left of the number. If the source is less reliable, write *LR*.
- Explain your answer on the line provided.

_____ **1.** an entry in a medical dictionary published in 1973

_____ **2.** an article published this year in a medical journal

_____ **3.** a recent magazine article titled "Helping Young People Deal with Diabetes," written by a doctor

_____ **4.** a Web page prepared by the American Diabetes Association

_____ **5.** an autobiography by a celebrity who has diabetes

_____ **6.** a 1985 encyclopedia article on the causes of diabetes

_____ **7.** an American Medical Association pamphlet called *Living with Diabetes* displayed in your doctor's office

_____ **8.** an online chat room discussion for people who have diabetes

_____ **9.** an interview with a doctor, published in a national newspaper this year, about diabetes treatments

_____ **10.** an interview, published in a national newspaper this year, with a woman whose grandmother died from undiagnosed diabetes

NAME CLASS DATE

for **CHAPTER 24: YOUR TURN 7** *page 660*

Prewriting: Taking Notes

DIRECTIONS Read your sources to find answers to the research questions you identified in **Your Turn 5.**

- Take notes on useful information on the sample notecards below.
- Use the same format for taking notes on other useful information.

SAMPLE NOTECARD

Subject of note: Source number:

Note written in your own words or author's exact words in quotation marks:

Source page number:

SAMPLE NOTECARD

Subject of note: Source number:

Note written in your own words or author's exact words in quotation marks:

Source page number:

NAME ________________ CLASS ________ DATE ________

for **CHAPTER 24: YOUR TURN 8** ***page 661***

Prewriting: Making an Early Plan

DIRECTIONS Use the following organizer to help you plan your report.

- Group your notes into sets that contain similar information. Write a heading for each set of notes.
- Number the sets to show the order in which you will discuss the information in your report.

This set of cards is about

#

This set of cards is about

#

This set of cards is about

#

This set of cards is about

#

This set of cards is about

#

This set of cards is about

#

NAME CLASS DATE

Prewriting: Outlining Your Report

DIRECTIONS In the space provided, create an outline for your report based on your notes and on the headings you created in **Your Turn 8.**

- Write your main headings next to the Roman numerals in the order you want to discuss them.
- Write your subheadings next to the capital letters under each main heading.
- Under each subheading, write details that explain the subheading.
- Add or delete numbers and letters as necessary for your outline.

My Outline

Topic:

I.
- **A.**
  - **1.**
  - **2.**
  - **3.**
- **B.**
  - **1.**
  - **2.**
  - **3.**

II.
- **A.**
  - **1.**
  - **2.**
  - **3.**
- **B.**
  - **1.**
  - **2.**
  - **3.**

III.
- **A.**
  - **1.**
  - **2.**
  - **3.**
- **B.**
  - **1.**
  - **2.**
  - **3.**

NAME ______________________ CLASS ______________ DATE ______________

Prewriting: Writing Your Main Idea Statement

DIRECTIONS Use the organizer below to help you write your main idea statement.

- Remember that this statement should serve as an umbrella for the Roman numeral headings of your outline.

Focused topic:

Main headings from outline:

I.

II.

III.

Main idea statement:

NAME ______ CLASS ______ DATE ______

for **REPORT OF INFORMATION** ***page 664***

Writing: Writing Prompts

DIRECTIONS Choose your own topic for your report of information, or use one of the following prompts.

CAREERS

Think of a career that interests you, and make a list of what you know about it and what you would like to know about it. Gather information about the career, using a variety of sources, such as Web sites, library resources, and interviews. Write a report about the career, and keep it in your personal portfolio for future reference.

SCHOOL

Your school mascot is everywhere—on team uniforms, at games, and in school publications. You are curious about how it was chosen. Research the mascot's history—when it was chosen, who chose it, and what it represents. Talk to the principal, teachers, coaches, and the librarian at your school. Also check other sources to find the meaning of the person, animal, or thing that represents your school. Then, write a report about the mascot for your school newspaper.

HEALTH

Vegetarian, high fiber, low fat, high protein—how can a person decide what eating plan to follow? Research one of these plans and write a report of information to present to your health class.

SCIENCE

You have recently visited, in person or online, a museum dedicated to scientific discoveries. Select a discovery that intrigues you, such as the development of the computer chip. Research the topic, and write a report of information to share with your science class.

SOCIAL STUDIES

On the calendar, you notice a number of holidays you have never observed. How and why are Flag Day and Arbor Day celebrated, for instance? Research the origins of some less familiar holidays, and write a report on your findings for your social studies class.

NAME ______________________ CLASS ______________ DATE ______________

for **CHAPTER 24: YOUR TURN 11** *page 667*

Writing: Drafting Your Report of Information

DIRECTIONS Complete the organizer below, and use it to help you write your first draft.

INTRODUCTION

▶ How will you grab your readers' attention?

▶ What will be your main idea statement?

BODY

▶ What is your first heading?	▶ What is your second heading?	▶ What is your third heading?
Supporting details:	Supporting details:	Supporting details:

CONCLUSION

▶ How can you restate your main idea?

WORKS CITED

▶ What sources did you use?

NAME ______________________ CLASS ______________ DATE ______________

Revising: Report of Information

DIRECTIONS Use this chart to help you improve your report of information.

QUESTIONS	DO THIS	CHANGES YOU MADE
1. Does the main idea statement cover all the important ideas?	☐ **Match each part of the statement** with a section of the report.	
2. Does the information in each paragraph support the paragraph's main idea?	☐ **Write an N** next to information that does not support the paragraph's main idea.	
3. Is the information in your own words?	☐ **Circle** sentences that sound as if someone else wrote them.	
4. Does the conclusion restate the report's main idea?	☐ **Put a check** next to the restatement of the main idea.	
5. Does a list of sources in the correct form end the report?	☐ **Check the format and punctuation** by referring to the guide on page 172.	
6. Does the list of sources contain at least three types of sources?	☐ **Count** the different types of sources.	

NAME ______________________ CLASS ______________ DATE ______________

Revising Practice: Report of Information

DIRECTIONS Below is an early draft of a report of information.

- Revise the paper to make it more effective, using the guidelines on page 669.

Despite its harsh climate, the Arctic is home to various animals with interesting characteristics and habits. Animals of the Arctic are specially matched to the region's extreme conditions. Brown or gray in the summer, the arctic fox turns white in the winter and so blends in with its surroundings year-round. The beluga whale is an expert at maneuvering around ice sheets floating in the Arctic Ocean. Sea otters, polar bears, and other animals endure the Arctic cold by eating a lot of food, which increases their internal heat production. Flowers are also found in the Arctic.

That concludes this report about the Arctic.

NAME ______ CLASS ______ DATE ______

for **CHAPTER 24: YOUR TURN 12** ***page 671*** **PEER- AND SELF-EVALUATION FORM**

Revising: Evaluating Reports of Information

DIRECTIONS Use the following questions to evaluate your report of information or that of one of your classmates.

- Answer the questions.
- Rate the parts of the report. The lowest score is 1, and the highest is 4.
- Make at least three suggestions for improving the report.

1. What important ideas are covered in the main idea statement?	**Rating** 1 2 3 4 ***Suggestion:***
2. What supporting information is provided for each paragraph's main idea?	**Rating** 1 2 3 4 ***Suggestion:***
3. What information in each paragraph needs to be rewritten in the writer's own words?	**Rating** 1 2 3 4 ***Suggestion:***
4. How does the conclusion restate the main idea?	**Rating** 1 2 3 4 ***Suggestion:***
5. Has the writer included a list of sources in the correct format at the end of the report? Which sources are not in the correct format?	**Rating** 1 2 3 4 ***Suggestion:***
6. What types of sources are contained in the list of sources? Are there at least three sources?	**Rating** 1 2 3 4 ***Suggestion:***

NAME ______________________ CLASS ______________ DATE ______________

Varying Sentence Beginnings

DIRECTIONS Revise the following passages by varying sentence beginnings.

- Look for sentences that begin the same way.
- Change one or more of these sentences by moving a phrase from the end of the sentence to the beginning. Add a comma after the phrase if necessary. Make your revisions on the passage.
- After you have completed this exercise, revise your report of information to vary sentence beginnings as directed in **Your Turn 12** on page 671.

PASSAGE A Dolphins are actually mammals, although they look like fish. Dolphins have a breathing hole on top of their skulls. Dolphins must breathe air and stay warm like all mammals. Dolphins make noises such as whistles and clicks to communicate and navigate under water. Dolphins whistle when they are excited or afraid. Dolphins use clicking sounds to catch fish for food. The clicks frighten fish and make them easy prey.

PASSAGE B Marie Curie won the Nobel prize twice during her lifetime. She won the Nobel prize for the first time in 1903. She shared the prize with her husband and another scientist for their discovery of radioactivity. Curie and her husband attempted to isolate certain radioactive elements after their original study of radioactivity. They wanted to determine the chemical properties of these elements. Curie and her husband needed to isolate the elements to do so. Curie's isolation of pure radium earned her a second Nobel prize. Curie focused on the development and use of X-rays for medical purposes in her later life.

NAME ______ CLASS ______ DATE ______

for **GRAMMAR LINK** ***page 672*** **ADDITIONAL PRACTICE**

Proofreading: Formatting Sources

DIRECTIONS Proofread the following sources.

- Revise the citations below, using correct punctuation and format.
- After you have completed this exercise, proofread your report of information to correct grammar, usage, and mechanics errors as directed in **Your Turn 13.**

Works Cited

(TV program): The Big Dig, The History Channel HIST, New York 1 Mar. 1999.

(Online source): Boston Harbor Islands National Recreation Area <u>ParkNet</u>. Dec. 1999. National Park Service. 15 Dec. 1999. <http://www.nps.gov/boha/>

(Magazine article): Calonius, Erik. 60 Fathoms Under the Sea <u>Fortune</u> 15 Apr. 1996: 128.

(Newspaper article): Goldberg, Carey. Stinking Heap in Boston Harbor Is Well on Its Way to Revival. The New York Times 27 June 1999: 12.

(CD-ROM): Gonsalves, Daniel, "Boston," <u>The New Grolier Multimedia Encyclopedia</u>. CD-ROM. Danbury: Grolier Interactive, Inc., 1993.

(Interview): Jacobson, Bruce, Telephone interview, 15 Dec. 1999.

(Book): Sullivan, Robert F. Shipwrecks and Nautical Lore of Boston Harbor. Chester: Globe Pequot Press, 1990.

(Encyclopedia article): Turner, Robert L., "Boston" <u>The World Book Encyclopedia</u>. 1997 ed.

NAME ______________________ CLASS ______________ DATE ______________

for **TEST-TAKING MINI-LESSON** ***page 674*** **PRACTICE**

Writing to Explain

DIRECTIONS Use the questions in the graphic organizer below to trigger ideas about your answer to one of the following prompts.

PROMPTS

- Think about an activity in which you compete. Why do you compete? What supporting reasons can you give?
- Think about how you use a computer. Why is it important to you? What supporting reasons can you give?
- Think about a favorite place you have visited—a museum, historic site, or amusement park. Why did you like the place? What supporting reasons can you give?

Questions	Reasons and Support
STEP 1: What is the prompt asking me to do?	
STEP 2: What is my answer to the prompt?	
STEP 3: Why did I choose this answer?	Reason 1: Reason 2: Reason 3:
STEP 4: What support can I give for each of my reasons?	Support for Reason 1: Support for Reason 2: Support for Reason 3:

Journal Warm-up: Persuasive Essay

Our school needs an alternative to study hall. Some kids do not understand why they are in study hall. They talk and make it impossible for others to concentrate. Why not let kids who do not want to study gather somewhere else?

The local soccer team needs business sponsors to provide new equipment and uniforms. This way, families would not feel pressured to "shell out" money so their kids could play. Team sponsorship offers advertising opportunities and a chance to show community spirit.

JOURNAL STARTERS

Write persuasively for five minutes, using one of these prompts.

- Do you think science fiction books are worth reading? Why or why not?
- Should students volunteer at soup kitchens? Why or why not?
- Persuade a teacher to give you more time to complete an assignment.
- Persuade your parents or guardians to let you try out for a team or a school play.
- You think hip-hop music is good, and your band director does not. Should hip-hop music be included in the school music program? Why or why not?

NAME ______________________ CLASS ______________ DATE ______________

Prewriting: Choose an Issue/State Your Opinion

DIRECTIONS Use the graphic organizer below to help you choose an issue and state your opinion.

- Brainstorm several issues about which you have strong opinions, or use the quickwrite sentences provided:

  If I were president, the first thing I'd change is ______________________.

  One thing that really bothers me about ______________ is ______________.
- List the issues along with your point of view on each. Circle the issue that you want to address in your essay.
- Then, write your opinion statement in the space provided.

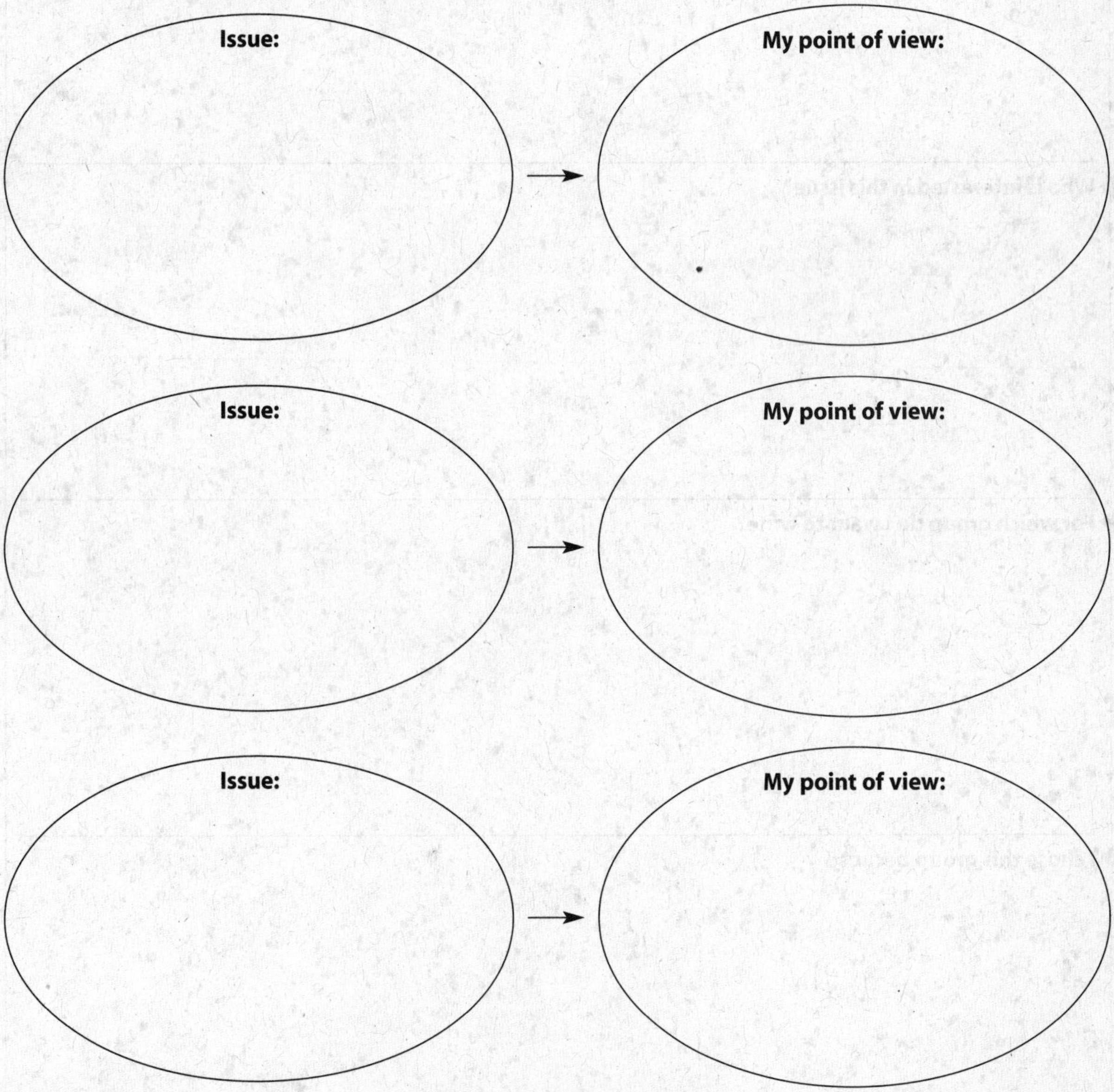

Opinion statement: ____

NAME CLASS DATE

for **CHAPTER 25: YOUR TURN 5** *page 699*

Prewriting: Identifying Your General Audience

DIRECTIONS Use the organizer below to help you identify your general audience.

- Think of at least two groups interested in your issue.
- Choose a group to address. State the reason or reasons you chose that group.

My opinion statement:

Who is interested in this issue?

For which group do I want to write?

I chose this group because

NAME ______________________ CLASS ______________ DATE ______________

Prewriting: Identifying Your Specific Audience

DIRECTIONS Use the organizer below to help you zero in on your audience.

My general audience is	They might disagree with me because	The age of people in this group would probably be	Other things I know about this group include

Based on the information listed above, my specific audience is

NAME ______ CLASS ______ DATE ______

for **CHAPTER 25: YOUR TURN 7** ***page 702***

Prewriting: Gathering Support

DIRECTIONS Use the chart below to help you gather support for your essay.

- Identify at least two reasons, along with supporting evidence, that will persuade your specific audience to agree with your opinion statement.
- In the last column, rate the overall strength of each piece of evidence as "okay," "good," or "best."
- After evaluating your supporting evidence, replace any evidence that you decide is too weak to convince your specific audience.

Reasons for my opinion	What supporting evidence will help me make this point?	How strong or weak is this supporting evidence? Why?	Rating
1.			☐ okay ☐ good ☐ best
2.			☐ okay ☐ good ☐ best
3.			☐ okay ☐ good ☐ best

NAME ______________________ CLASS ____________ DATE ____________

Telling the Difference Between Fact and Opinion

DIRECTIONS Identify each of the following statements as either a fact or an opinion.

- Write *Fact* after each statement that can be proved true. Write *Opinion* after each statement that expresses a personal belief and cannot be proved true.
- Briefly explain your answers on the lines provided.

1. Our city's population increases every year.

____

____

2. The $21 million renovation plan for Lane Middle School includes a new gymnasium.

____

____

3. The *Ledger*'s story about Mr. Martinez, the basketball coach, was the best article in the whole newspaper.

____

____

4. The Olympic games are held every four years.

____

____

5. For three years in a row, the school swim team won the state championship.

____

____

6. I think our community places too much emphasis on sports and not enough on the arts.

____

____

7. I believe that schools should never cut extracurricular programs like sports, music, or drama.

____

____

8. Every student should participate in at least one sport during the school year.

____

____

Writing: Writing Prompts

DIRECTIONS Choose your own issue for your persuasive essay, or use one of the following prompts.

WORKPLACE

Your neighbor travels frequently and is looking for someone to collect her mail and check on her home when she is gone. You have told her you are interested, but she is hesitant to hire you because she has always had someone a little older do the job. Write an essay to persuade your neighbor that you are the best person for the job.

SCHOOL

School starts each day at 7:30 A.M. and ends at 2:00 P.M. The school board has been considering a recommendation that middle schools in the district start later. The new hours would be 9:00 A.M. to 3:30 P.M. How would you feel about this change in schedule? Write a persuasive essay for your school paper explaining and supporting your point of view.

HEALTH AND SAFETY

There are many cyclists in your community. Some ride to work, some make deliveries by bike, and still others ride bikes just for pleasure. All agree that riding a bicycle is sometimes dangerous. Write a persuasive essay for your local newspaper that addresses the need for bike lanes on major streets.

SCIENCE

A group of students in your science class would like to help local efforts at cleaning up a nearby wetlands area. School policy does not permit students to become involved in outside projects without teacher supervision. You believe your science teacher is the perfect sponsor for the project. Write a persuasive essay on the issue to present to your science teacher.

SOCIAL STUDIES

In national elections, the United States has a lower voter turnout than most other democratic nations. Voter turnout is low, especially among people 18 to 24 years old. Write an essay for your social studies class addressing the importance of voting.

NAME ______________________ CLASS ____________ DATE ____________

for **CHAPTER 25: YOUR TURN 8** ***page 704***

Writing: Drafting Your Persuasive Essay

DIRECTIONS Complete the graphic organizer below, and use it to help you write your first draft. Use additional paper if necessary.

INTRODUCTION

▶ How will you grab your reader's attention?

▶ What is your opinion statement?

BODY

▶ What is your first reason?	▶ What is your second reason?	▶ What is your third reason?
What evidence supports that reason?	What evidence supports that reason?	What evidence supports that reason?

CONCLUSION

▶ How will you restate your opinion?

▶ How will you summarize your reasons or include a call to action?

NAME ______________________ CLASS ______________ DATE ______________

for **FCAT PREP MINI-LESSON** ***page 707*** **PRACTICE**

Writing a Position Paper

DIRECTIONS Use the graphic organizer below to help you organize thoughts for a position paper.

- Choose one of the writing prompts below, and take a position on the issue.
- Identify the issue, the two options, the purpose, and the audience.
- List the benefits of two options related to the issue, using the memory strategy THEMES: **t**ime, **h**ealth, **e**ducation, **m**oney, **e**nvironment, **s**afety.
- Decide which option you support. Then, list the drawbacks of the option you do not support, again using the memory strategy THEMES.

PROMPTS

- Noise and loitering have become problems at the public library in your community. The city council is considering whether to keep the library open to all or to limit its use to people with library cards. Which option do you support? What are the benefits and drawbacks of the option you support?
- All seventh-grade students at your middle school have the same lunch period. Next semester, however, lunch periods may be mixed, with students from all three grades eating together. Which option do you support? What are the benefits and drawbacks of the option you support?

Issue: ______________________

Two options: ______________________

Purpose: ______________________

Audience: ______________________

	OPTION #1	OPTION #2
Benefits (time, health, education, money, environment, safety)		

Option I support: ______________________

	OPTION I *DO NOT* SUPPORT
Drawbacks (time, health, education, money, environment, safety)	

NAME ______________________ CLASS ______________ DATE ______________

for CHAPTER 25: YOUR TURN 9 **page 710**

Revising: Persuasive Essay

DIRECTIONS Use this chart to help you improve your persuasive essay.

QUESTIONS	DO THIS	CHANGES YOU MADE
1. Does the introduction grab the audience's attention?	☐ **Put stars** next to interesting information.	
2. Does the introduction have a clear opinion statement?	☐ **Underline** the opinion statement.	
3. Does the essay include at least two reasons that logically support the opinion statement?	☐ With a colored marker, **highlight** the reasons.	
4. Does at least one piece of evidence support each reason?	☐ **Circle** the evidence. ☐ **Draw a line** from the evidence to the reason it supports.	
5. Does the conclusion include a restatement of the opinion?	☐ **Put a check mark** next to the restatement.	
6. Does the conclusion include a summary of reasons or a call to action?	☐ **Draw a wavy line** under the summary of reasons or call to action.	

NAME ______ CLASS ______ DATE ______

Revising Practice: Persuasive Essay

DIRECTIONS Below is part of an early draft of a persuasive essay.

- Revise the essay to make it more effective, using the guidelines on page 708.
- Look for problems with the introduction, with the opinion statement, and with support.

Soon we may be going to school year-round. Many teachers think more school days are needed to cover material. I do not like the whole idea for these reasons.

Summer is the only time many people have to spend more than just a few hours each day with their families and friends. My family, for instance, goes away to a lake every summer.

Summer is also a great time to try new things. A new activity is easier to learn when you have time to focus on it.

NAME ______ CLASS ______ DATE ______

for **CHAPTER 25: YOUR TURN 9** ***page 710*** **PEER- AND SELF-EVALUATION FORM**

Revising: Evaluating Persuasive Essays

DIRECTIONS Use the following questions to evaluate your persuasive essay or that of one of your classmates.

- Answer the questions.
- Rate the parts of the essay. The lowest score is 1, and the highest is 4.
- Make at least three suggestions for improving the essay.

1. How does the introduction grab the audience's attention?	**Rating** 1 2 3 4 ***Suggestion:***
2. What is the writer's opinion statement?	**Rating** 1 2 3 4 ***Suggestion:***
3. What reasons does the writer use to support the opinion statement?	**Rating** 1 2 3 4 ***Suggestion:***
4. What evidence supports each reason?	**Rating** 1 2 3 4 ***Suggestion:***
5. How does the conclusion restate the opinion?	**Rating** 1 2 3 4 ***Suggestion:***
6. What summary of reasons or call to action is given in the conclusion?	**Rating** 1 2 3 4 ***Suggestion:***

NAME ______________________ CLASS ______________ DATE ______________

Clichés

DIRECTIONS Revise each of the following passages by replacing the clichés with original, forceful words or phrases.

- Cross out the words you need to replace, and write new phrases above them.
- After you have completed this exercise, revise your essay to eliminate clichés as directed in **Your Turn 9.**

PASSAGE A The Leeville Town Council is trying to decide whether the town should continue to support the Weekend Youth Recreation Program. Without this program, many kids in this town would be bored stiff. Why would the town council want to take away a sure thing? The town council members obviously don't have a clue about how we feel.

PASSAGE B For a while, it seemed that Americans were like eager beavers trying to save the planet. Everywhere you went, the message was clear as a bell. "Don't waste energy." "Recycle." "Don't litter." I think the message has been lost in the shuffle. For example, has anyone else noticed how much paper and plastic we throw away at lunch in the cafeteria? It's time for a wake-up call.

PASSAGE C Membership in student organizations should not depend on grades. This school policy should be changed. The idea behind the policy is that if students want something, they'll work like crazy to get it. The idea is not totally off base. However, there are some kids who work like horses but still get poor grades. These students need a place where they can be the cream of the crop.

NAME ______ CLASS ______ DATE ______

Proofreading: Using Comparatives

DIRECTIONS Proofread the following passage.

- Underline the incorrectly used modifiers, and give the correct form of the modifier.
- After you have completed this exercise, proofread your persuasive essay for errors in comparatives as directed in **Your Turn 10.**

If Principal Hughes and the PTG (Parents Teachers Group) have their way, Carter Middle School students will have to wear uniforms next year. The more I think about it, the more clearer the picture is in my mind. Everybody will wear dark blue pants or skirts, white shirts, and green sweaters. We will all kind of blend together, like melted crayons. Nothing could be more scarier! Since how I dress expresses who I am, I think that we students should not be forced to wear uniforms. Uniforms are much more bad than a strict dress code.

At assembly last week Mr. Hughes said that students will have a more easy time focusing on schoolwork if they don't have to worry about what to wear. In other words, uniforms will make the school a gooder environment for learning. Uniforms aren't going to change how we feel about one another. Even with uniforms on, we'll still get along weller with some kids than others. I think Mr. Hughes underestimates us by suggesting that we judge one another by our clothes. Some students may think that way, but most of us are more smart than that.

Write letters to Mr. Hughes and the PTG to explain why uniforms are a less good idea than a dress code. Ask your families to attend the PTG meeting and vote against the school uniform proposal. Let's stand up for what we want: No uniforms!

Journal Warm-up: Print Advertisement

Last year Cameron played sick whenever he had a math test, Dion doodled instead of reading, and Jorge gave up on becoming a veterinarian. This year, thanks to New Horizons Tutoring, Cameron, Dion, and Jorge made the honor roll. New Horizons—ordinary kids, extraordinary accomplishments.

The Joneses just carpeted their whole house. So did the Millers next door, the Judds down the street, and the Carreros one block over. Underfoot Flooring's rock-bottom prices let everyone keep up with the Joneses!

JOURNAL STARTERS

Write persuasively for five minutes, using one of these prompts.

- Persuade a friend to buy a bag of raisins from you to support the school band.
- Persuade a family member that one kind of computer is better than another.
- Convince your classmates that exercise is important for good health.
- Persuade someone to switch to your type of shampoo.
- Tell people your age why they should read more books and watch less TV.

NAME ______________________ CLASS ______________ DATE ______________

Prewriting: Choosing a Product, Finding a Market

DIRECTIONS Use the graphic organizer below to choose a product or service for your advertisement and to identify a target market.

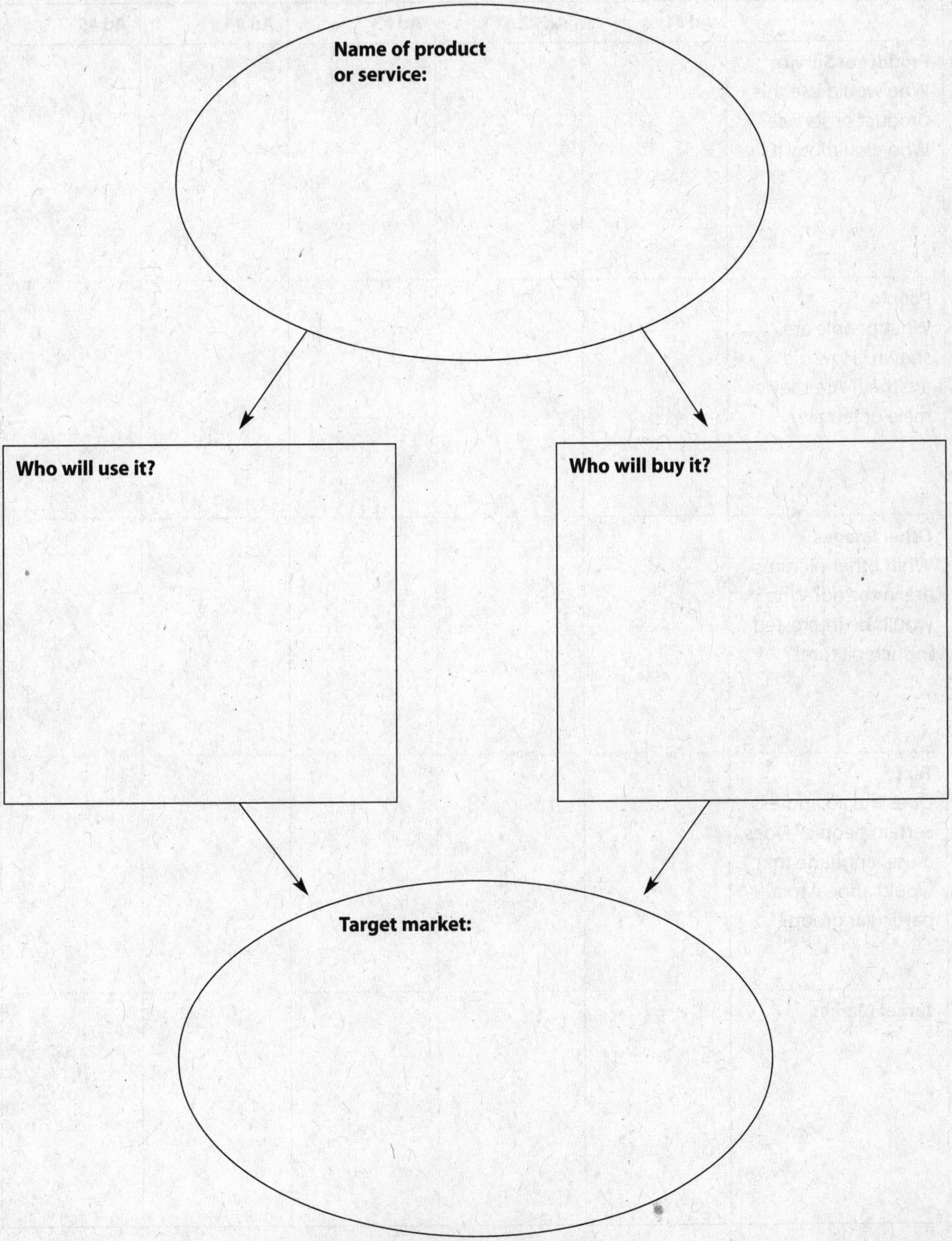

NAME ______________________ CLASS ______________ DATE ______________

Analyzing Target Markets in Advertisements

DIRECTIONS Find five print ads, and use the graphic organizer below to help you identify the target market of each.

	Ad #1	Ad #2	Ad #3	Ad #4	Ad #5
Product or Service Who would use this product or service? Who would buy it?					
People What people are shown? How old are they? Are they male or female?					
Other Images What other pictures are in the ad? Who would be interested in such pictures?					
Text Does the ad address certain people? Does it use language that would appeal to a particular group?					
Target Market					

NAME ______________________ CLASS ______________ DATE ______________

Prewriting: Analyzing the Target Market

DIRECTIONS Use the graphic organizer below to help you analyze your target market.

- Circle the most important need. You will use it to choose your persuasive technique in **Your Turn 6**.

Product or Service

Target Market

Needs	**Wants**

Prewriting: Choosing a Persuasive Technique

DIRECTIONS Use the graphic organizer below to choose a persuasive technique to use in your advertisement.

STEP 1

Identify target market's main need.	
Pick a persuasive technique that addresses this need.	☐ Bandwagon ☐ Emotional Appeal ☐ Snob Appeal ☐ Testimonial ☐ Plain Folks
Explain your choice.	

STEP 2

Test the persuasive technique by writing the technique and the need in the blanks.	Will ______________________ make the target market believe they will ______________________?

NAME ____________________ CLASS ____________ DATE ____________

for **CHAPTER 26: YOUR TURN 7** ***page 734***

Prewriting: Writing a Slogan

DIRECTIONS Use the graphic organizer below to write a catchy slogan for your product or service. Try using alliteration or rhyme to make your slogan easy to remember.

Persuasive technique I have chosen ____________________

WHAT I WANT TO SAY ABOUT MY PRODUCT OR SERVICE

MY SLOGAN

Prewriting: Choosing an Image

DIRECTIONS Use the graphic organizer below to choose an image for your print ad that fits the persuasive technique you have chosen.

- After deciding on the details for your image, sketch a draft of the image in the box.

Subject I have chosen:

What the subject will be doing:

IMAGE FOR MY AD

What else I will include in the image:

Colors I will use to convey emotions:

NAME ______________________ CLASS ______________ DATE ______________

for CHAPTER 26: YOUR TURN 9 **page 735**

Prewriting: Planning the Text

DIRECTIONS Use the graphic organizer below to plan the text of your ad.

	Text of Ad
Description of product or service (sizes, colors, business hours, key features)	
Reasons to buy the product	
Action readers should take (Where can they buy the product or service? What is their next step?)	

NAME ______ CLASS ______ DATE ______

for PRINT ADVERTISEMENT page 736

Writing: Writing Prompts

DIRECTIONS Choose your own product or service for your print advertisement, or use one of the following prompts.

WORKPLACE

A local business sponsors a "Coats for Kids" drive every winter to collect warm coats and jackets for children in your community. You are in charge of advertising the drive at your school. Create a print advertisement urging support for the coat drive.

SCHOOL

The school orchestra has decided to hold a special concert to raise money for new instruments. The orchestra hopes to draw a large crowd for the event. Create a print advertisement for your school newspaper encouraging students and teachers to support the orchestra by attending the concert.

WORLD LANGUAGES

A local travel agency is sponsoring a two-week trip to Montreal, Canada, for students studying French. The trip will strengthen students' language skills because everyone will speak only French on the trip. Create a print advertisement about the trip for publication in the school's monthly newsletter to parents.

MATHEMATICS

Studies have shown that many young people lose interest in mathematics during their middle-school years. To build young people's enthusiasm for math, this summer your school is offering a special math program to help those who are falling behind. Create a print advertisement about the program for a flyer to be sent home to parents.

LITERATURE

You recently read a book you couldn't put down, and you think others your age would enjoy the book as much as you did. The local library has agreed to post an advertisement about the book on its bulletin board if you will design and write the ad. In your ad, include information about the book as well as reasons people should read it.

NAME ______________________ CLASS ______________ DATE ______________

Writing: Drafting Your Print Advertisement

DIRECTIONS Complete the graphic organizer below, and use it to help you write your first draft. Use additional paper if necessary.

SLOGAN

IMAGE

- Subject supporting persuasive technique:
- Colors:

TEXT

- Tie-in to persuasive technique:
- Description of product or service:
- Reasons to buy the product or service:
- Action reader should take:

NAME ______ CLASS ______ DATE ______

for CHAPTER 26: YOUR TURN 11 *page 741*

Revising: Print Advertisement

DIRECTIONS Use the chart below to help you improve your print advertisement.

QUESTIONS	DO THIS	CHANGES YOU MADE
1. Would the image catch a reader's attention?	☐ **Note** two things about the image that would make a reader look at it.	
2. Is the slogan catchy and memorable?	☐ **Underline** words that have rhyme, alliteration, or some other catchy element.	
3. Does the ad have a clearly defined target market?	☐ **Write down** two specific things that point to the ad's target market.	
4. Does the ad provide a clear description of the product or service?	☐ **Put a number** next to each fact about the product or service.	
5. Does the ad clearly tell readers what action to take to buy the product or service?	☐ **Place a check mark** by the information that tells the readers what action to take.	

NAME ____________________ CLASS ____________ DATE ____________

Revising Practice: Print Advertisement

DIRECTIONS Below is an early draft of a print advertisement.

- Revise the ad to make it more effective, using the guidelines on page 739.
- Look for problems with the slogan, with the description of the product, and with the action readers should take.

LunchTote

a better way to carry your lunch!

Next time you take your lunch to school, use LunchTote. You're too cool to carry your lunch in a boring brown paper bag. LunchTote comes in six cool colors and is available now.

DATA

- two sections keep food hot and cold
- high-tech material used to construct
- six colors available
- leakproof
- expandable

NAME ______________________ CLASS ______________ DATE ______________

Revising: Evaluating Print Advertisements

DIRECTIONS Use the following questions to evaluate your print advertisement or that of one of your classmates.

- Answer the questions.
- Rate the parts of the advertisement. The lowest score is 1, and the highest is 4.
- Make at least three suggestions for improving the advertisement.

1. How does the image catch a reader's attention?	**Rating** 1 2 3 4 ***Suggestion:***
2. What makes the slogan catchy and memorable?	**Rating** 1 2 3 4 ***Suggestion:***
3. What is the ad's target market?	**Rating** 1 2 3 4 ***Suggestion:***
4. What facts are used to describe the product or service?	**Rating** 1 2 3 4 ***Suggestion:***
5. What action should readers take to buy the product or service?	**Rating** 1 2 3 4 ***Suggestion:***

NAME ______________________ CLASS ______________ DATE ______________

Using Emotional Language

DIRECTIONS Revise the following sentences by replacing ordinary words with more-emotional ones.

- Cross out the words you want to replace, and write the new words above them. You may delete or add other words if necessary.
- After you have completed this exercise, revise your print advertisement to add emotional impact to your words as directed in **Your Turn 11.**

1. The new movie *Video Kid* is good. It has action scenes and interesting characters. You will be sorry if you miss it.

2. Flashback stores carry all the latest styles. If you are looking for clothes, shop at Flashback.

3. Everybody is talking about the online magazine *CyberTeen.* Teens like it.

4. This Saturday only, soccer player Benita Sanchez will be at the Sportz Shop on Michigan Avenue. She will sign autographs and demonstrate her on-field moves.

5. The rides at Waterpark USA are exciting. Water can be fun.

6. Tired of dull pencils? Get a SharPoint mechanical pencil and never use a pencil sharpener again.

7. You could put mustard or mayonnaise on your sandwich, but why would you when you could use Zesty Sauce instead? It's tasty.

8. You will never have fly-away hair again if you use Foundations Hair Spray. Give your hair the support it needs.

NAME ______________________ CLASS ______________ DATE ______________

for **GRAMMAR LINK** ***page 742*** **ADDITIONAL PRACTICE**

Proofreading: Punctuating Possessives

DIRECTIONS Proofread the following passages.

- Underline the words that need an apostrophe, and write the words correctly.
- After you have completed this exercise, proofread your print advertisement for errors in possessive nouns as directed in **Your Turn 12.**

PASSAGE A Book lovers, share your passion! Volunteer at the toddlers story time, 10 A.M. every Monday, Wednesday, and Friday at Los Angeles Drop-In Childrens Center. Read aloud your favorite stories from the centers huge collection, or bring books from home. The delight on kids faces will make your day! To become a volunteer, attend the readers-group training session any Saturday at noon. Your adventure in reading can begin as soon as Mondays session.

PASSAGE B Need answers to lifes hard questions? You're not alone. In todays world, students questions about important issues challenge many teachers. How do you respond to your class tough questions? You could adopt the Socratic method of answering with a question. Better yet, share some of Socrates and other philosophers wisdom with the video "Philosophy for Teens." The ideas of historys greatest philosophers have never been easier to understand.